"This book has opened my
never dared to ask a mediun
to see how much the spiri ... actually
willing to communicate and educate us."

Wendy F. from Cleveland, Ohio

"I feel the reading of this book was divinely guided. My beloved son, Joshua, had just passed away suddenly at too early an age. Little did I know there is a complex, coordinated, and well-structured system to our soul's evolution."

S. Scott, Kentucky

"I have never read this genre of book. I am an avid fiction reader. Yet as I read this accounting of the few years in the lives of these people and tested the believability of the situation which caused confusion, fear and reactions to these events, it rang true to me. Beverly's situation of her mental health concerns and the treatments offered by the medical professionals for her behavior was typical for this age. In the past ages the treatment might have been to use leeches, exorcism, electric shock or lobotomies whichever was in vogue at the time. It made me wonder what will the future treatments be? Back to the book ... It made me really think about the interconnectability of our lives. Whether I believe, or not, in past lives or soul fragments, it got me to think about my life. I have come away with a desire to look at my current relationships and interactions from a new view, due to this book's material. This book was provocative on many levels, a thought inducing writing."

D. Anderson, Albany OR

Thank you so much for purchasing:

We got It All Wrong:
death and grief, heaven and hell, and mental illness

From our
Soul Evolution: the Invisible Structure series

As an added bonus we have prepared a *FREE* 30-page PDF companion workbook that you can use to work along as you read through the book.

GET WORKBOOK AT:
HTTP://BIT.LY/SESERIES

check us out.

An Extraordinary Journey
BOOK ONE

We got it All Wrong:

death and grief
heaven and hell
and mental health

HAFEMEISTER & MCBRIDE

SE Imprints
Cincinnati, Ohio

We Got It All Wrong:
death and grief, heaven and hell and mental illness
by: Hafemeister (Beverly) & McBride (Kym)

Cover design by: BorsukDesign.com
Cover Image: Shutterstock.com/Jagerion Caiph
Edited by: PaperRavenBooks.com

Publisher:
SE Imprints, Cincinnati, Ohio - (513) 464-9782
www.SEImprints.com
SEImprints@gmail.com

Publisher's Cataloging-In-Publication Data
(Prepared by The Donohue Group, Inc.)

Names: Hafemeister, Beverly. | McBride, Kym. | Todeschi, Kevin J., writer of supplementary textual content.
Title: We got it all wrong. Book one, Death and grief, heaven and hell and mental illness / Hafemeister & McBride ; foreword by Kevin J. Todeschi.
Other Titles: Death and grief, heaven and hell and mental illness
Description: First edition. | Cincinnati, Ohio : SE Imprints, [2016] | "An extraordinary journey." | This title is book one of the series: We got it all wrong -- per author. | Companion workbook also available (9780997958836).
Identifiers: LCCN 2016953373 | ISBN 978-0-9979588-0-5 (print) | ISBN 978-0-9979588-1-2 (ePub) | ISBN 978-0-9979588-4-3 (mobi) | ISBN 978-0-9979588-2-9 (audiobook)
Subjects: LCSH: Hafemeister, Beverly. | Spiritualism. | Death. | Psychic ability. | Future life. | Loss (Psychology) | Mental illness.
Classification: LCC BF1261.2 .H37 2016 (print) | LCC BF1261.2 (ebook) | DDC 133.9--dc23

Printed in the U.S.A.

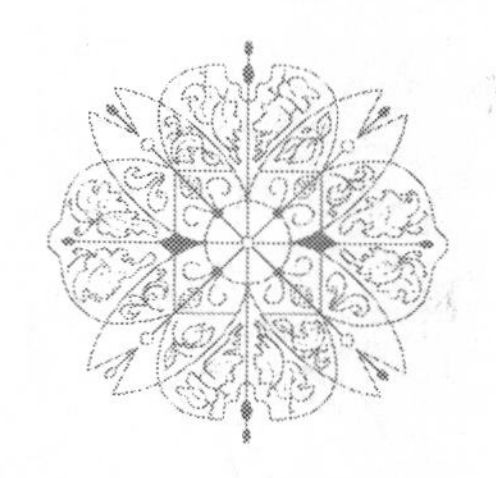

Dedications

Beverly:

To Sis
My wise role model of a lifetime
And
To The Rest Of The Family
Past, Present, and Future

Kym:

I'm dedicating this book to the greatest teachers in my life:

My grandmother, *Mary Loftus Middleton*
who showed me that a woman can be powerful and
a bit crazy at the same time and it's okay.

My mom, *Maureen Middleton McBride Maxwell*
who challenged me to fight to find my own power.

My sister, *Traci McBride*
who from the day she came into the world
demonstrated that power was not a dirty word.

My teacher and mentor, *Linda Schiller-Hanna*
who gave me the tools to let my own power and
light shine out into the world and
find my own joy in the process.

I bow to each and every one of you.

Table of Contents

Foreword

Anyone who is interested in the survival of the soul, the possibility of communicating with a loved one who is deceased, psychic awakening, or healing past-life issues will find an interesting read in *We Got It All Wrong: death and grief, heaven and hell, and mental illness.*

Originally coming together as a team—one serving as a medium, the other in the role of healing recipient—McBride and Hafemeister have culled together information from some of their transcript sessions that deal with elements that all of humankind faces at one time or another: our individual spiritual journey, how personal trauma and unresolved issues can somehow "fragment" the soul, dealing with and working through grief, the influence of past-life experiences on the present, and ultimately "why are we here?" and "how does the Universe operate?"

Along the way, as readers share the personal journey of the co-authors, they will discover the reality of spirit guides, the ultimate benevolence of the Divine, and the fact that the world may be on the verge of an enormous paradigm shift.

Kevin J. Todeschi

Executive Director & CEO, the Edgar Cayce work, Association of Research and Enlightenment (A.R.E.), www.EdgarCayce.org

Author of 25+ books, including: *Edgar Cayce on the Akashic Records, Edgar Cayce on Vibrations, Contemporary Cayce, The Best Dream Book Ever, and Dream Images and Symbols.*

Soul Evolution; the Invisible Structure is the partnership company of Beverly Hafemeister and Kym McBride. In this collaboration, they write books together that educate, enlighten and open a conversation with their readership on varied topics of the evolution of the soul.

Their body of work should be seen as a stepping stone to redefine long held beliefs on a myriad of topics that limits our awareness of the invisible structure, which is in place so that all souls progress through to enlightenment.

Through their trademark interview style, their work opens a two-way street to a team of instructors (in spirit) who teach higher concepts of the ways this invisible structure is formed to lead all souls back to Source. These are not religious constructs, but spiritual. For some, these spiritual concepts have a tendency to bump-up against many religiously taught dogma.

This is first book in the series:

We Got It All Wrong:

death and grief, heaven and hell, and mental illness. (2016)

It will be followed by:

We Got It All Wrong: Companion Workbook (2017)

We Got It All Wrong: Book 2 (Fall 2017)

Contact: SoulEvolutionSeries.com

SoulEvolutionSeries @gmail.com

How to Navigate This Book

The Tandem Journeys of Two Women

The client, Beverly, who is on a personal growth journey, realizes she needs help to unravel her problems. She seeks out an advisor to pinpoint reasons for malfunctions in her life so she can engage again in endeavors she values.

Kym, the medium, is on a professional journey to increases her metaphysical knowledge base. She has access to her spirit teachers, but only in working with clients is her mind broadened by the clients specific situations which uncover long-hidden viewpoints and answers from the other side.

Two separate journeys are happening simultaneously.

Overseeing and coordinating their own individual paths are the two spirit guides. Level-headed and rather straight laced is Timingo, the perfect guide for a medium. In contrast, Beverly's guide, known here as Cherith (and perhaps Bob), is a master of disguises with a droll sense of humor and is the perfect compliment to an uptight client. Both guides are constant, behind-the-scenes companions and coaches and an integral part of the women's invisible structure throughout this series.

Neither guide is a fan of the lecture type mode of teaching hence the conversational/transcription style that the book is written in. The guides believe in description, demonstrations, and allowing time for their charges to experience the teachings. This style of teaching necessitates dripping in the women's understanding on an as-needed-basis over the years to keep them expanding their experience and comprehension.

What Is The Invisible Structure?

It is a beautiful, organized, multifaceted support system which surrounds all people at every stage of life. This structure's parameters guide you back to Source which is achieved through levels of enlightenment (knowledge).

Just as in a building blueprint, much of the important components needed for a structure to function smoothly, such as; plumbing, electrical wiring, and temperature control, is tucked in out of sight within the walls, hidden but very much a part of the daily workings.

Similarly, the spiritual invisible structure appears mostly concealed, yet includes:

- People (spirit guides, soul fragments, family)
- Governance (levels, outlines)
- Organizations (souls, soul clusters)
- Routes (pathways to specific experiences)
- Laws of Nature (gravity, energies)
- Multi-dimensional tasking: (mediums, crossings, warriors, psychics)

How Information Was Obtained For This Book

Ability definitions:

- Psychics are clairvoyant. They can tell what's going to happen in your future. They usually get information from spirit guides, angels, ascended masters, etc.
- Mediums are also psychic. In addition, their fine-tuned ability allows them to see and channel information from dead people who have crossed over.

- Another type is dubbed ghost whisperers. They are not psychic (seeing the future) but they see earthbound ghosts, but not crossed spirits.
- Some mediums and psychics have the additional ability to see ghosts. Some do not.

How a medium works:

- Mediums connect to the energy of the deceased. Some do this by asking the client to say their name along with their deceased friend's name back and forth three times. With this method both of their energies are connected.
- Because mediums are channeling the dead, they can pick up feelings, personality, words, and many times actual inflections of the person's style of speaking as well as their physicality.
- Mediums receive communication through their senses; touch, sight, hearing, taste, and smell. Additionally for many it's more difficult to explain the ability called *knowing*. Knowing is information about someone or something without the benefit of hearing words or seeing a vision. It just pops in your head.
- Some mediums feel things in their own body that the deceased person's body felt, such as physical impairments, illnesses, and the cause of their death. It passes through the medium's body, so they can describe or interpret it for the client. When doing this in the book the wordage is, "I feel…"

Another important term is the use of the *validation chill*. This is a way the guide acknowledges that the medium properly described and interpreted the information sent. It's best described as a chill that comes from inside the body outward. Unlike a chill from a cold blast of wind, this chill is not a reflex being done *by* the medium. It's done *to* the medium. This validation chill isn't given on every bit of information. Thank goodness or mediums would be perpetually uncomfortable! Not all mediums experience a validation chill.

Prologue

Are you ever really aware when a life changing situation crosses your path? It's the *moment just before* everything you know to be is irrevocably changed?

I had one of those profound moments. Armed with only 200 bucks in my pocket, I moved to Ireland with an ill conceived plan to make a life for myself there as a photographer while I searched for the family of my dead great-uncle. I never knew him but loved him wildly after finding his powerfully passionate and loving letters in my family genealogy. After weeks on the west side of Ireland living in one perilous situation after another, I finally limped to his town on the east side of the island. After continuous days of illness and malnutrition, I was nagged relentlessly by my spirit guide to get out of my sick bed and drag myself to a nearby restaurant for food. It turned out that the very first person I talked to gave me the information I had traveled over 3,000 miles to hear. My great-uncle's granddaughter was still living in the town and worked at the top of the hill.

As I took long, yet weak strides up the hill, I became more revived as I was struck with the clarity of that moment. I knew everything I was and knew about myself up to that point was going to change in the next moment. And it did.

So I know what I mean when I ask you, "Do you know the moment *just before* everything you know about your life, is irrevocably changed?" The clarity of these type of moments are profound but a bit rare.

On the other end of the pendulum, there are the more common life changing moments that arrive yet you are completely oblivious to it at the time. These experiences also have an enormous effect on your life with equal profoundness.

Meeting Beverly Hafemeister was one of those oblivious moments.

I'm glad it wasn't the rarer *moment just before* situation, for I don't know if I would have had the courage to move into the next moment with her if it had been. To compare the *moment just before* and my meeting with Beverly, I would liken our interaction to the repetitive, consistent, dripping of water, one drop at a time, onto a rock. It appears to have no effect at all, but over a long duration of time the water etches, grooves, changes the rock bit by bit in immutable ways, reshaping it with each drop.

In 2009, I was asked to do a short talk at an event for the Edgar Cayce's Association of Research and Enlightenment (A.R.E). I was given a 15-minute slot in a program by psychic Linda Schiller-Hanna. Excitement was bubbling inside of me. I thought it was because of the killer presentation I was ready to give, but could it have been the excitement of my soul, knowing that a woman who would change the direction of my life had arrived in the audience at this perfect exact moment? This change would not be in the next moment, like meeting my long-lost family in Ireland. Instead, the paradigm shift would cautiously sneak up on me. It took over a few years to fully grasp me in its clutches, but once it did, it wouldn't let me wiggle free.

The shift snuck up on Beverly, too. At the A.R.E. event, the inciting moment had not yet hit her, but it was silently, doggedly rolling down the tunnel, picking up speed as it moved toward her. Yet, she wouldn't be able to outrun it like Indiana Jones. This was her *just before moment,* of which she was unaware.

The boulder which would cause her shift was *grief*—unrelenting, soul wrenching grief—which could not be rationalized, soothed, or cried out. It literally would knock the wind out of her. She was going to drown in it.

Grief was not new to Beverly. She endured intense grief in her life: the loss of her marriage, the tragic death of her mother, her father dying shortly after her mom, and watching her sister slowly being debilitated by Parkinson's disease. Beverly knew grief. She had experienced grief with the loss of her farm and her beloved horse Rudy, but not like this.

A month after our mutually unnoticed A.R.E. meeting, the inciting incident hit Beverly head on. She had fits of weeping and heavy depression followed by feelings of weighty despondency. She couldn't eat or care about anything. She was in the throes of this grief and didn't know how to process this loss, let alone deal with it.

Her beloved mentor, counselor, and the most inquisitive platonic friend she had ever encountered, Hal, had died. But he didn't *just* die. She found out that h*e died a year ago.* The loss was acute and compounded by mixed feelings that he abandoned her. She had felt that their connection was so deep that she would surely know when he took his last breath. But she hadn't known. Her self-abusive reprimands yelled at her that she should have known! Why didn't he let her know he was critically ill? When he did die, why didn't he come to her in her dreams? She wondered if she was as important to him as he was to her. This was further exacerbated by knowing that her dream of meeting up with him again and sharing stories of their adventures over the last 40 years of separation, would now never happen. She had hoped that they would have had time. Now his death meant the complete severance of this relationship, which was especially hurtful since he didn't even wave goodbye.

She didn't know where to turn. These intense feelings of grief weren't getting better; they were getting worse. She had little family to help her or advise her. She was 71 years old and she was virtually alone.

Beating upon her mind was one thing, and one thing only. She couldn't let it end, not like this. She had to talk to Hal again. But how?

She had heard of mediumship, and although she hadn't experienced it, she felt she had to give it a try. She remembered the talk a few months back, from a medium at the A.R.E. lecture. She found the promotional flier from the event and called Mrs. Schiller-Hanna, hoping that Linda might be able to help. Linda referred Beverly to a medium named Kym McBride, who just happens to be me.

At last, the invisible connection of our paths was in motion and the slow methodical, plop, plop, plop began.

Beverly contacted me for a telephone appointment. Unbeknownst to us both, we simultaneously walked through the door of massive change. No fanfare. No clashing of cymbals, lightning strikes, or music playing. Nothing to signify to us that this was the massive shift in our lives. Wouldn't it be nice for the Universe to have given us such clear signs?

Our working intent was to find relief for Beverly from her sadness and some sort of closure to this loss. We had no idea how this clear-cut need was the tipping point to the greatest adventure of our lives. It wasn't a sprint or a fast race. It was a long journey of unfolding thoughts, ideas, and insights that were taught to us by a large cast of characters over a series of readings. Of course, the adventure did start with Beverly meeting her dear friend Hal again, which allowed her intense grief to wane. But we were soon introduced to many others, some of Beverly's family and a few famous drop-ins, who wanted to give us their viewpoints on the invisible structure that houses the evolution of all our souls. This was not a topic to which we even thought there were answers.

But this journey would be fraught with many terrifying experiences that would challenge Beverly's sanity and would make her bout of grief look like a day in the park. Beverly's life became a torment that required great knowledge and understanding to bring her back to balance. My part of this tandem journey is channeling the insights and connecting the dots for both Beverly and you, our readers. With each drip, drip, drip of information we are given in these readings, I hope to piece together the information into a congealed form to understand that our lives are influenced by many invisible energies and agendas. For some extremely sensitive people, this influence has often been misidentified as mental illness, and has caused many a person to choose suicide for relief. We hope this book will supply some answers that could save another, just like it did Beverly.

I'll hand over the rest of the story to my writing partner, Beverly, who serves as the experimental "lab rat" in this book.

Hello Reader, I'm Beverly.

I told Kym it was okay to see me as a lab rat who had signed up for an interesting journey that included communication with the other side by way of spirit guides, past lives, ghosts, and crossed-over spirits; all of whom, unbeknownst to me, were active parts in my current life. Lab rats are trapped in the midst of the whims of someone else's agenda and that's exactly how I felt on many occasions during this long journey of discovery.

My personal journey is recorded here. I wish it were not, because I'm a private person. However, I see how my life since early childhood has always included a sincere spiritual quest. Experiences contained in this book are wider and wilder than I wish, but I realize they are a vehicle for other seekers. Therefore, I share my experiences, happy or sad, with others who yearn for deeper understandings beyond religious tenets.

Grief of all kinds, I now realize, has had a huge imprint on my life. My intense sadness for my friend required a lot of soul searching to cleanse away debilitating habits and alarming lifelong repercussions. Not facing practical daily matters was tripping me up big time, I learned. Also, I stepped into using an old psychic tool, automatic handwriting, that was meant to close the gap between dimensions, but instead opened me up to situations that could serve as a cautionary tale for others. The ripple effects of sorrow continues to live on, and to this day still pops its ugly head up in unexpected places.

As the reader, you're invited along on my unique journey for the sole reason of discovering concepts of which you may have been unaware; yet, these very concepts support your path every day. You will find, as Kym and I did, that we go through life unaware of our largely-invisible spiritual support system no matter what our preferred religious dogma is.

To help you navigate this book, we have recorded each reading and transcribed the words using the initial of the speaker before their statement. For example: *(K) Kym, (B) Beverly, (T) Timingo, (C) Cherith.*

We welcome you as a fellow traveler on our journey of discovery.

Kym & Beverly

Where Are You, Hal?

November 28, 2009, Beverly's Mindset:

I awoke knowing that today is the day I made a ten o'clock telephone appointment with Kym McBride, a medium, to connect me with my deceased friend, Hal.

By eight-thirty I'm already dressed and pacing the floor in a cold sweat. What am I so nervous about? Decades ago, I had a psychic do a couple of readings for me to see what the future held. She gave me accurate information that gave me a heads-up concerning my future, but I don't remember being as panicky as I am now.

Maybe the difference is I never asked to speak to a dead person before. I don't know what to expect with a psychic who is also a medium, one who channels the deceased. It all sounds so creepy. What if Hal can't be found? Or worse yet, I once heard of a medium who reached the intended person, but the spirit refused to turn around to talk to the medium's client. What if Hal doesn't want to talk to me? After all, my time with him is only a two-year blip cruising by his life's radar screen. His impact on me was profound, but it doesn't necessarily mean that I, over a dozen years his junior, was memorable in his life.

I watch the hand of the clock sweep around minute by minute. Shivering with fear I sit down in front of the window in my workroom. Maybe he won't remember who I am? I'll feel like a fool. Oh, what a bird-brained idea this was. Whatever possessed me to set up this appointment?

At precisely ten o'clock my phone rings. I hesitate. Whether Hal wants to hear from me or not will make all the difference in the world. I believe I'm standing on the precipice of a life-changing event. I let the phone ring twice more before I pick up the receiver with a shaky hand. I hear the trembling fear in my voice as I say, "Hello."

It's Kym McBride from Cleveland. After a few cheerful words of greeting to allay my anxiety, she begins.

Beverly (B), Kym (K), and Hal (H)

K: Beverly, I know you want to speak to your friend Hal, so say your name and his name back and forth three times so I can intertwine your energies.

B: Beverly … Hal …

K: Hal has his arms around you and me to bring us together. Earlier this morning prior to my call Hal popped in to urge me to phone you immediately. He knew you were getting cold feet as you sat at home alone, waiting and watching the clock. I resisted his pushing. I always start at the scheduled time, so I told him, "Hold your horses, Mister. This is my rodeo!"

So Beverly, would you like to know what Hal has to say, or do you want to ask him some questions first?

B: He was right. I was losing my nerve and was teetering on the edge of cancelling for fear he wouldn't want to talk to me. Why don't we let him talk?

H: [*calmly and lovingly*] Why is she so upset?

K: [*to Hal*] She's saddened to discover that you've passed on.

B: Yes, I just recently learned of his death, but he died over a year ago!

H: It's always been inevitable.

K: How very philosophical you are. He's telling me of your time together. Did you know him before he was a minister in your local town?

B: No. Before studying for the ministry, he had a career as a college physics teacher, if that's what you mean.

K: Hal was talking about the ministerial work when it was relatively new for him. As your minister, you and he were on intimate terms. I feel a depth in private, personal talking and sharing. He said your time with him was intense, yet brief.

B: Yes, he was a pivotal, important friend to me while I dealt with the death of my parents and my divorce. Fortunately, I was surrounded by several wise friends during that critical, awful period. He and my sister were my primary resources for advice. Life was harsh, yet it was a wonderful time of personal growth.

K: Right, that's why it feels so intimate. I was trying to get a handle on your relationship. Your friendship was as impactful for him as it was for you. He wondered about you, often even asking others about you when he was reassigned to other churches. Although he never let you know directly, you really never left his heart and mind.

H: Beverly, were you ever able to allow love back into your heart?

B: Your question confuses me. When a beloved person dies like a parent or friend, they remain in my heart. I don't boot them out.

After the departure of my husband, in that aspect of my life, I needed to concentrate totally on supporting myself. Like many divorced women, my heart went on hold. If the question is, "In the thirty-five years since Hal's church reassignment, have I ever met a man whose company I enjoyed equally well?" then the answer is "No." Frankly, he set a high bar.

K: Sorry to interrupt, but I'm getting all these physical sensations. Hal had cancer on the upper right side of his body in a shoulder muscle near his collarbone. The cancer spread, especially in his right arm. It was not genetic. The cancer was slow when it started. He was aware of it. He knew. He says, "How I died wasn't important."

B: Oh dear! Was it melanoma? He told me his doctors always needed to watch his skin.

I drove up to Michigan for a high school reunion weekend, the summer of 2004. I attended Hal's church service, which was the last time I saw him. While at the pulpit he rubbed his upper body and was wincing in pain, so I was suspicious he was dealing with a serious health problem.

After the church service ended I, found myself in a strange conversation. Unwittingly, chatting with Hal and some congregants, I turned the conversation to Dr. Jack Kevorkian, who advocated and practiced an extreme right-to-die opinion. A fortnight earlier in my out of state home, I had caught the tail end of the national news about Kevorkian demanding the right to use a particular church for one of his clients over the adamant objections of its pastor. Innocently mentioning this news item, I sensed a cool reaction to my comment, but didn't understand why.

Weeks after our short reunion, it dawned on me all the particulars of the news story pointed towards it being Hal's church. I realized that Hal was the minister who was forced to tussle with Jack Kevorkian's extreme goals. I thought, "Boy, Kevorkian does not know my buddy!"

Whatever possessed me to pick that hurtful topic of all things? I felt terrible for not putting those unpleasant pieces together sooner. Now I realize it was my friend who, while facing his own mortality, had to resist this clumsy champion of the right-to-die movement. I had ambivalent feelings about my visit since we did not have an opportunity to exchange any private words. When I got in my car to leave, I cried, knowing I would never see or talk to my friend again. And I never did.

K: There was such an acceptance of his diagnosis. He didn't give himself over to the illness. Hal was focused on the fact, as his death approached, that he had completed so much. He was very fulfilled, organized, and ready to leave. I do not feel a struggle. I do not feel he fought down to the last moment like so many men do. There was a peace about it.

H: Bosom Buddy, I was so okay with it. I was prepared and ready.

K: For him, being prepared meant everything. He had plenty of time to deal with all of his arrangements. In the end, it was the most peaceful transition you can imagine. He wants you to be peaceful too. He did have time and he was aware. It wasn't a shock to him.

B: He was an energetic person, so fully into this world.

K: He did enjoy this world! Having his body not react the way it normally did, especially his right arm and shoulder, gave him a lot of pain, and it was frustrating and annoying. He feels he did everything he was supposed to do. He didn't give in to the disease. He did treat it, and accepted it but didn’t go through the stage of anger. If that was the way he was to go out, then okay. He was grateful for the time he was given.

B: When he was alive, occasionally I thought he came to me in my half-awake state where I would feel his presence. Frankly, that’s what surprised me when I heard he died. I wasn't aware of his passing! As I think back to that winter, I was in my own depression, dealing with my own physical health, so maybe I missed his calling card. Since I had no sign of his departure, I assumed he was alive. Maybe when the time came he decided there was no hurry to tell me. I wasn’t ready to hear bad news.

K: As you started to talk he said, “She wasn't ready.” When he could connect to people, he knew you were not ready. It wasn't the right time to inform you.

B: I can believe that! When I finally learned he was dead, extreme grief overwhelmed me. I didn’t know how much of my overpowering reaction was just me already physically not feeling well, how much of it was the loss of my great friend, or how much of it was for some other reason entirely.

H: Beverly, you're so intuitive and so connected to me that a part of you did know, which probably lead you unconsciously to your depression. Yet I didn't come to you in a very clear way because you weren't ready. You needed more time. I believe you're now strong enough. I believe you are ready.

K: I had a similar situation with my stepfather. Max died suddenly in his sleep at the age of 54, without a day sick. It was such a shock that my grieving mother fell into a terrible depression. Prior to me becoming psychic, Max came to me in a dream and stated he could not go to my mom because it would not help her—it would hinder her. I didn't understand at the time, but he was right. Mom was too fragile to get this clear connection. At the time she might have made the decision to follow him through suicide.

B: Yes, I see the similarities in our loved ones refraining from contacting us until we are ready to move forward. It's funny, maybe I unwittingly started to get the ball rolling after all when I went to find him!

In my case I had been obsessed with the idea of sending Hal, whom I had not contacted in decades, a recording of Dr. Bruce Lipton's *The Biology of Belief*. Hal was the perfect person who'd love to hear this validation of the "love field" which he himself preached decades prior. In tracking down his address through church headquarters, I was informed Hal had died over a year earlier.

H: I choreographed all those details!

B: That rascal! And I truly believe it now. Wow! What a brilliant scheme to nudge me gently into news I didn't want to hear. No wonder Hal has been on my mind, especially since I had to drive through his home state on business recently. Maybe he even arranged that job?

K: He's chilling me all over in validation.

H: I'll be there to hand guide you through some difficult times yet to come. I'll help you through this as I've helped before.

B: Oh, that sounds ominous. Surely there are other past lives in which we've crossed paths.

H: Many! And many more to come!

B: [*chuckling*] I thought this was my last trip!

H: No! We have so much more to experience together in different ways.

K: He comes back with you often in all of your lives. Even if it's for a short time, as in this life, it's always in profound roles. He doesn't just pop in and out like an acquaintance, he really loves you much more than as your employer or friend. You were lovers at one time, which is the basis of the intimate friendship.

He's showing me a real fun life with you as caring, loving, playful siblings where you developed this supportive be-there-for-each-other feeling. Many lifetimes of different types of love have been played out in different ways. You two wanted to experience the whole gamut with each other. It explains the intense bonding for you even though contact in this life was a short period of time. You're remembering the remnant feelings from other lives. I think he was your father at one point. He has many different kinds of love for you. I'm getting fatherly, then suddenly it's very brotherly, then as a lover. All very interesting.

B: A person needs more than one lifetime to develop all of those emotional variations. Is there anything I can do for him now?

K: He says to just be with him. I see him sitting on the sofa with an arm around his pal—just being together, talking as the closest of friends. He wants to be in the quietness of your everyday life, for you to share with him. He says he's there with you more now than he could ever have been in life.

H: Don't be sad. You got more quality time with me than most people did.

B: Yes, I appreciated that gift. What I miss most now is when he attended annual pastors' school and brought back his class notes that we freely questioned and pondered its meanings.

H: What I'd really like you to do is make me a constant visitor. Set a special time for you and me, perhaps the end of the day, to just be. Talk to me out loud, I will answer.

B: Maybe this is where my fears come in. Am I ready?

H: You are ready. That's why I made it happen. I want to have a different type of relationship with you now.

B: Yes, it would be nice to reprise some of those earlier days when I shared with him my out-of-body meditation experience. He sat wide eyed, listening to me with a twinge of jealousy surrounding him. Now he's had his own ultimate out-of-body experience!

K: He's sitting there laughing and chuckling at you. I just feel his huge smile, and tears of pride in his eyes. He's very proud of who you are, how you experience this life, and how you experienced him.

He's aware of your emotions and smiles tenderly towards you. I'm trying to put words to his feelings, which are pretty intense. He loves you a lot so I'm basking in his love for you. He's making me get all teary eyed. He's very excited about this meeting. He says, "Don't fall into grief over my death. It's just an experience."

B: Yeah, I'm okay with that intellectually, but putting it into practice is much harder!

K: He says he's been with you. I see you sitting at a table crying and him standing over you, putting his arms around you, trying to calm you. His heart breaks when you cry. He's been through this with you before. He doesn't want you to go into the darkness of grief.

He's reminding me of an experience when I lost my mother this year. We had great closure in our relationship, but I would have uncharacteristic outbursts of crying. I didn't know where they were coming from. One day, in meditation, I started having another outburst.

All of a sudden I saw Jesus standing before me. I'm Catholic-based, but I haven't been practicing on any level for many years. Jesus asked if he could have the ball. I said, "What ball?" I looked down and in my hands was a ball. He repeated, "Can I have your ball?"

I realized that the ball signified my mom. "No, it's my mother. I don't want to give her up."

He asked if I could open my heart and send all of my grief into the ball. I ended up doing it. Then he again asked if he could have the ball. Again I said, "No, this is all I have left of her."

He said, "Please. Grief was not meant to be a long-standing emotion. It was meant to be a short, temporary emotion that allows cleansing to happen in our bodies. To hold on to grief long term is destructive and will not do any good."

Finally, he convinced me and I gave him the ball. He took the ball. I have never seen such love expressed. He looked at that ball and put it on the ground.

At first I was confused and said, "Wait a minute! What are you going to do with my mother?" I thought he was going to crush her.

Jesus knelt down in front of the ball and put his hands together in prayer. He looked up to the heavens and said, "Father, please take away this child's sadness and grief for the loss of her mother. And unleash Maureen's goodness and absorb it into the heavens. Anything that was not good, allow it to dissipate."

As Jesus prayed over my mother's ball, it cracked open and the most beautiful butterfly emerged and flew up to heaven and was absorbed. He asked me to do this same ceremony at her funeral. At the funeral, we replicated this ceremony by releasing live butterflies. It was the most profound experience for all in attendance!

H: You can do this too. Give your sadness and grief for me to Jesus. And allow all its goodness to be absorbed into the Universe. Permit it to happen. Beverly, you hold grief. You need to release it. I don't want your feelings for me to be destructive to you. I want them to be inspiring to you. I'm going to be with you and do it with you. Just give your ball of grief to God.

K: Or whatever your belief system determines, Source, Jesus, Buddha, Allah ...

H: You're going to feel such relief. The crying and sense of loss will stop because you've allowed *my* goodness to be released. When one grieves deeply over a long period of time, they hold back a part of their loved one's soul. It needs to be released to become part of the Source again.

K: He's a loving, loving soul.

B: I feel honored to have known him.

H: I'm just as honored, if not more.

K: He's telling me that you had a great impact on the man he was. You can take pride in his work as if it was your own because that's how much of an impact you had. He's a very giving man.

You don't understand the impact on him also. He's showing me that his intense feelings of love and protectiveness for you was profound. He hurts when you hurt. Oh, he's going to make me cry!

B: He affected other people that way too. Being his secretary brought me much closer to knowing him than the average congregant. I could see how genuinely he empathized with other people's problems.

H: Beverly, you allowed me to be more.

B: Yes, when we worked together, we were forthright with each other. He once told me he was a better minister for having known me. So his saying how I impacted him sounds just like him.

K: I am glad he was able to verbalize directly to you in this life. Not many people get that opportunity. Or rather, they don't usually take the opportunity to give this kind of insight of their feelings to those who need to hear it.

B: I'm curious. How does he occupy his …? I want to say time, but I know he isn't "in time" on the other side.

K: I've never had anybody ask that question. You know what's so funny? He's chosen to work with new ministers. He's saying some of these new ministers are unable to help young people who are coming to them because of the pastors' lack of life experience and skill in handling situations. Hal's chosen to work through them because of the struggles they have in this new society. Damage is being done because of their ineptitude. He spends a lot of time in that capacity.

B: Does that mean on Earth with the living or between lifetimes or both?

K: Both. He's very attuned to new ministers on Earth. He also works with ministers on a much more global scale.

B: Oh! That reminds me. When he first became a minister, his first congregation stated they were pleased to have an older person who was more tuned into real life rather than the typical young person they were assigned just out of seminary. His response was that the gift this small church gave was to help educate new pastors into their roles as wise counsellors in the lives of people. Mutual growth was the goal.

K: I'm glad he was able to get that idea across.

B: Over three decades ago, as church secretary, I witnessed his concern about the well-being of ministers. In fact, several ministers scheduled counseling time with him for personal advice. I believe that he's still working on the problems of caregivers. He often said, "Who ministers to the minister?" For him, I was that person.

K: On the other side, he's going to continue his work with young ministers.

B: There's one last loose end I need to tie up. With my suspicion in 2004 that my visit might be the last time I would see Hal, I brought along the cross he had given to me as a remembrance gift when he was again assigned to another church in a different part of the state. He had kept the cross hidden in a drawer for years. It had special sentimental significance for him from his post World War II Army days. After the war, he was living with a local civilian family in their bombed apartment in Germany, and during this time he received a lovely cross. He suspected the cross originally belonged to a nun and was somehow "liberated" from her during the war.

The artfully crafted cross was a gift I treasured. Yet, in accepting the gift, I vowed to myself to return it one day because it was part of Hal's life. I was its temporary custodian. After much debate with myself, I decided it was time to part with it.

As it turned out we didn't have a private word. I certainly wasn't going to shove it back into his hand coldly without expressing my gratitude and thanks. What kind of friend would do that? So instead I took the cross back home and mailed it to him along with a note.

B: Did Hal get the cross I returned? Did it arrive okay?

K: He's clutching something in his right hand and feeling happy.

B: Oh good! Well Kym, Hal is a remarkable person. I'm glad you got to meet him.

K: Yes, he is remarkable. Do you have any more questions for me?

B: No, thanks for everything.

Beverly's Personal Journey:

After this session I felt stunned, relieved, overwhelmed, and overjoyed.

On a personal level, I felt happy to know that our appreciation of each other was mutual. Furthermore, the fact that we continually arrange to come back into each other's lives as helpers is refreshing and comforting as expressions of a deep loving commitment. No wonder in this life I moved quickly from fearing conversations with him, to appreciating his sterling thoughts and qualities. Our bond wasn't a figment of my imagination. At the time of his assignment to another church, I hadn't immediately grasped the compliment he gave me on his last day of his tenure at our church when he left a note on my desk that read, "Thank you for making me think." Apparently he had enjoyed our talks, too.

On the abstract level, Hal said many curious things in this highly detailed reading that I wanted to know more about, such as when he said that it was "inevitable" he would die first. Did he mean because he was older, or because it has something to do with a past life? He seemed to know a lot about our past lives, and I wondered how many details he knew regarding the future. Then there was all that business about the active connection between my world and his. I had no idea there was mundane, ongoing contact with spirits who seem eager to assist. I guessed I better start saving up for my next session with Kym.

Kym's Professional Journey:

When I started working with Beverly, I was in the professional medium seat. I had a built in emotional distance from the work, but I quickly saw that I too was being taken on a journey. Throughout these sessions, I was getting specific details that would change how I saw my work, and that would allow me to understand so many of the complex variations of what our guides call "the invisible structure."

I have been working as a professional medium for many years now, and I've talked to close to 1,000 dead people. I see many holes in my understanding, because I have not had the time to pay better attention to the nuances of these spirits. When I'm working in a reading, I'm always working against the clock. I have a client who is literally paying me by the *minute* for my words, so I am always aware of the tick, tick, tick of the clock. I have to give my clients a constant stream of information, so I take no time to ponder the tiny details of the spirit that has come to talk. I don't feel I have the luxury of such observation. Details might be coming out of my mouth, but they're not coming *from* me, but rather *through* me. Therefore, I'm not connected to the information the way I would be if it were my own mind developing the words.

I will be letting you, our reader, in on the new awareness I'm finding in the sessions. I want you to understand what skills and abilities a spirit has, whether they are a crossed spirit, a ghost, or our own spirit guides. I want to understand how they all fit into this invisible structure of the evolution of the soul.

In our first meeting, Hal told us much about the abilities of a spirit on his level. I'm going to re-state them for ease of organizing these pieces and parts. I'll do this whenever I can so we, you the reader and I, can learn in a simple and succinct way.

Recap: Crossed spirits still have their personality, intelligence, sense of humor, and style of speaking. Their feelings of love do not stop. They still have their free will. These souls can decide if they feel a loved one is ready or not to know things about them and their transition. They can manipulate situations to bring a living person into an awareness, like when Beverly got a job that would require her to drive through Hal's home state, which led her to finding out about his death. Human connection with living people is important, since a crossed spirit can work with earthlings in assisting them with problems or jobs, such as Hal with the ministers. They are privy to some of the future, like when Hal knew Beverly was heading for a very difficult time in the coming months. They are also privy to some of the past. Hal could tell Beverly about some of their past lives together.

So far, what I understand is that a crossed spirit has all the same abilities we have in the body, but they are more fortunate, because they are not dragging around a body that needs upkeep! They still work and help others, but they don't have to make a living. Other than that, as I see it, we're pretty much the same.

When I shared my experience of Jesus and the ball of grief, I was taken aback by the deeper knowledge Hal shared. "The crying and sense of loss will stop because you've allowed *my* goodness to be released. When one grieves so deeply, over a long period of time, they hold back a part of their loved one's soul."

What a whole different perspective on grief. Many clients, family, and friends think that if they are still grieving for a loved one then they are keeping them alive somehow, but in essence, they are actually holding them back. Powerful! This will forever change the way I grieve.

The information in this session that really blew me away though, was that Hal was working. Information of that nature had never come up in a reading before. Firstly, because no client had ever asked, and secondly, no spirit had ever offered up that scrumptious tidbit. I really had never thought about it before. I bet when my mom showed up at the pearly gates she was gobsmacked! She always said she couldn't wait to sit on a cloud with a harp and pluck the days away. I bet she was surprised there was still work to be done!

I found this work aspect of Hal's existence to be fascinating and it led to all kinds of questions in my head. Questions which he answers in the next chapter. He also dropped a few hints as to how our lives are planned down to the small details. It's a great opportunity for me to share a teaching Timingo gave me a few months back, that we refer to as "the outline."

Personal Growth Questions:

1. Do you always assume that pivotal people in your life have to be long term associates? Name someone whose short duration relationship with you has nevertheless had a major impact on your life.
2. Why was Hal so anxious to reconnect? What's his motive? Was he lonesome, sorry for Beverly, following orders? Was he being smothered by Beverly holding on to the ball of grief, refusing to release his goodness back to God?
3. Did you notice how the crossed-over soul chooses to work in jobs related to his earthly occupation? Why do you think that is?

Am I Talking to Dead Air?

March 25, 2010, Beverly's Mindset

Today's my birthday, so I decided to give myself the present of scheduling a conversation with Hal by way of Kym. It's been four months since we've talked and I'm feeling somewhat better about Hal's death. The surprising thing is how lax I've been about setting an intention to communicate with him. Hollow is the way I describe these last few months. I guess it's what the radio broadcasting industry calls "dead air." (Oh man, what a bad pun!) Quiet is quiet, empty is empty, and I'm tired of it. It's hard for me to sense whether anyone is here or not when I can't hear or see them.

Instead, I have many questions bubbling in my head. With Hal's passion for physics, is he learning anything new in that field? Does living where he is now, on the other side, afford him any new, special talents or abilities? I can't imagine what it's like to live without a physical body. This time, when the phone rings, I notice that I'm not nearly as nervous as I was four months ago.

Beverly (B), Kym (K), and Hal (H)

K: Happy birthday Beverly. If you're ready to start, please say your name and your friend's name three times.

B: Okay, thanks. Beverly … Hal …

K: Prior to starting, I was meditating. An unknown man came in and is now standing to my right. He's so tall that he's actually leaning over me. His dark brown hair is balding, his eyes sparkle, and his smiling laughter is jovial, but a little silly. Do you know who he is?

B: I can't think of who he might be. Is it my spirit guide?

K: [*to the man*] Does she know you?

Man: Of course she knows me. Just call me "Bob." [*saying his name in a decidedly monotone way*]

K: He says, the name isn't important. He just wants to be involved in this process.

Hal is much smaller than Bob, but then everyone is. The white-haired Hal gives me an educated feeling, a gentlemanly demeanor, and brings you a huge smile. He's very different from jovial Bob on my right. Were Hal's eyes light, like blue?

B: Yes, but more grayish.

K: Hal's just beaming as he says, "Happy birthday. Of course, happy birthday!" There's a gentle lovingness to him. What did you want to ask him?

B: Do I understand Hal can see and hear me when he wants to? Can he read my thoughts or do I have to speak orally?

K: Nobody's ever asked that question before.

B: I am amazed no one has ever asked!

K: Yeah I am too, now that you've asked it. Let's find out.

H: Yes, I see you anytime I want. As for reading your thoughts, it's not as you think. I read your energy. Your thoughts and your feelings are all mixed together. When you're lonely, sad, or thinking about me, I feel it and know it. Your thoughts and feelings are all energy, so I am aware.

B: Before I talked to you Kym, I was watching a PBS TV program by physicist Dr. Brian Greene called *The Elegant Universe* about string theory. If Hal were here in the room at the time, could he hear and watch it with me?

H: Yes, I can be there while you're watching the show about quantum physics if I focused my attention on it.

B: On the show they were talking about membranes, as if all Earth has layers like slices of bread. There were many times during this PBS program I wanted to pick up the phone and ask him to please explain it to me. Kym, you might remember that his first career was as a physics teacher, the second was as a minister.

My question really is where in the heck is Hal residing? Is he out past Pluto, or is he on one of those nearby membranes? Or, has he been right here on Earth this whole time?

H: In your limited concept, where I am is not part of your galaxy. Picture a large circle. Place a very small circle inside of it. The Milky Way galaxy is in this tiny orb inside of a bigger orb, the Universe. I'm at the edge of the bigger orb, you guys are in the smaller orb!

B: Does he remember being in the big orb before? I'm not sure what to call it.

H: I remember all of the times I've been here, now, but as an earthling, no.

B: Does he remember it or does he see his Akashic records, the etheric field of imprinted past events? If so, could he see mine?

H: Yes, I can see my own records, but it's not my place to get anyone else's. If you were with me, we could look at each other's records.

B: In the short time we had together, it was exquisitely timed. Circumstances allowed us to have quality time to develop a deep friendship.

K: He's sitting next to you patting your hand. He's sending his energy through his hand into your hand.

B: As to comfort, this kid would prefer a pat on the head! [*laughing*]

H: [*smiling*] Our time together was perfect.

K: Your love for him, his love for you, are duly matched.

B: Was it planned in advance?

H: Yes.

B: That's comforting.

H: Yes, it was planned in advance down to the details. Not being here with you currently was planned that way too.

K: [*seeing and feeling as a vision flashes past me*] This is blowing my mind! I'm seeing this is such an organized structure!

B: Obviously to make the whole Universe work, there would have to be coordinated structures all over the place. I'm finding peace with myself because I finally understand Hal and I are living in a different phase now, since we're on two different planes.

K: Good to know your grief has subsided somewhat.

B: I gathered from our first conversation with Hal, there was an invitation to continue learning with him, but I haven't figured out by what means.

K: You're one of the few clients who doesn't just get a reading and take it only for face value. You are finding ways to enhance the information and learn more. That's great!

Right now, you think you can only talk to Hal via me, but that's not true. By learning meditation, you can talk to him directly. Mediation is not just getting "blank" for relaxation like most people think. It can be used to converse with crossed spirits. Bev, you're learning more. I'm proud of you.

Hal is bringing up a new topic. Have you ever heard of the White Brotherhood?

B: I'm not sure.

K: The White Brotherhood consists of spirits who came from the top of every walk of life: healthcare professionals, scientists, philosophers, and religious leaders of all denominations and belief systems. They work with Earth people on various matters at a high level. Hal says he has assisted them in some manner as part of his work on his current level.

I've worked with the brotherhood in my healing program, called *MAP: The Co-Creative White Brotherhood Medical Assistance*. That's interesting that he's working with them. From what I know they are a very powerful group.

Now Hal is bringing up a teacher/professor who was his mentor. Do you know this person?

B: If it's who I think, I know of him, but not personally. Recently, I have been listening to old tape recordings of Hal's sermons where he mentioned Harry Emerson Fosdick, who was a liberal preacher Hal admired.

K: I felt a validation chill when you mentioned Rev. Fosdick.

B: Yes, in fact I went to the library to borrow his book and am reading it now.

K: Hal's validating that Rev. Fosdick was the man he meant and to let you know he's aware of the simple daily things you're reading. It's another way to reinforce that he's involved in your current life.

B: Yes, no doubt it was also a surprise for him to see I kept so many old recordings of his sermons and classes. It was good stuff! I hope that's okay.

H: Good! That's very okay. Love should not be hidden, feel inappropriate, or shameful.

K: He's coming from a very philosophical point of view.

B: I feel very protective of him.

K: Hal just took his hand and put it on your face as you mentioned being protective of him. I think he's protective of you too.

B: I hope he doesn't come when I'm clipping my toenails or brushing my teeth!

K: [*laughing*] He pops in often when you're just sitting quietly reading or listening to music. I almost feel at this point he doesn't want to disturb you, but just to be with you. He looks very comfortable, like it's his home. Your love keeps him connected, alive, and happy.

H: That's enough for me until you join me.

B: He's probably seeing how boring I am. [*laughing*]

H: Don't think that! I love your mind.

B: I'm sorry I can't hear him directly. [*Kym is repeating his words for Beverly*]

H: I hear everything you say so I reply back. You do hear me, you just don't realize it's me. You react to what I say, but may not know I generated the thought. If you want to make a specific date, I'll be there. For example, every night at eight o'clock, let's talk. Make that intention in your mind and I'll be there. Talk out loud. Over time, you'll begin to feel my presence. Of course, I'm there much more than just at this meeting time.

K: To help you connect, make it a routine. Sense how you feel. Soon you'll recognize this connection. Anytime you want him, bam, he's there. You don't need me to connect for you. In the beginning if you try to connect more loosey-goosey, your focused intention is not as strong, so it will be harder without a set schedule.

B: I'll think about it. Tell him I'll call.

K: Please understand you've got the ability to make the connection yourself!

B: When listening to Hal's old recordings, I admired how he could speak both formally from the pulpit and humorously in informal class settings. Not everyone has that talent. I hold him in high regard.

K: Hal holds you in high regard too. You underestimate your value in his life.

B: Yes, he said I helped him to be a better minister. I know that's true, but I never seriously believed it until now.

One other item, has he found time to come to the biofeedback sessions I'm doing? If so, what does he think of them?

K: He understands it more now. I do see him sitting in a room reading a newspaper next to you while you are attached to the biofeedback machine.

B: Does that mean he's bored?

K: No, he's just being a comfort to you.

B: It's twenty-first century medicine. My friend Gloria studies and works hard at her biofeedback skills. It's a lonely path because the traditional medical profession is so enamored by the chemical approach to health, they are rarely receptive to energetic modes of diagnosis and healing. It drives her nuts because she sees the benefits, especially since it's so non-invasive.

K: He understands energy more on the other side than he did here, biofeedback included. It's all part of energy: thinking energy, feeling energy; everything is energy. To him now, it's almost completely normal. He's happy that you're interested in scientific subjects.

B: I'm sure he is. As for physics, I never retained much information. In fact, physics interests me a lot more now than when I was in high school.

H: Don't negate the value of what you are learning here. For what's coming down the road for you, this knowledge will be needed to understand how things work for the growth of your soul. Plus, this pre-information will give you a leg up when you get to the other side. [*Reader, we had no idea what he meant at this point, but soon it would all hit the fan.]*

B: Soul growth sounds good to me! The advantage of living a long time is seeing my growth. Frankly, it's a wonderful bonus to be able to look back at my life and realize how much I've changed.

K: Do you want to live longer?

B: Not a heck of a lot! [*laughing*]

K: That was my own curiosity. I know my mom was depressed and wanted to die for a long time. I think it was triggered by the loss of my stepdad, so I was curious to talk to someone in her same age bracket to see how she compared. At your age, do you want this life to be done?

B: No, just because I'm in my seventies doesn't mean I'm finished with life!

It was my grief over the death of Hal that deflated me. Death sounds like a silly word now since he's very much alive. Prior to his passing I had always been a news junkie. After his death, I had to shut off all words and only listen to classical music. My brain was on overload. Long-buried memories and feelings were overflowing. I wanted to hide from the world. Any hopes or dreams of talking with him again were finished, but now I know differently.

K: You've described the grieving process for many. It's good to articulate those feelings.

B: My motivation for looking for Hal all started when I wanted to send him a scientific discussion by Dr. Bruce Lipton.

I wanted to get his take on the talk. I'll assume now that Hal was with me while I listened long before I knew he was dead. Well, I'd still like Hal's feedback.

K: He's showing me a man sitting on a bench, left of center. I think he's referencing Dr. Lipton. He sees this guy favorably because he has a forward way of thinking.

B: Dr. Lipton is an epigeneticist researcher talking about energy. I'd never heard anyone else speculate about a *love field* except Hal several decades before. My understanding of the love field is that it is an area of predictable loving responses of inhabitants dwelling therein. So, to my ear, here was a cellular biologist using virtually the same notion. I was amazed!

K: I'm being told Dr. Lipton doesn't have it all figured out, because there's so much more to discover.

While Hal was on Earth, he tried to think bigger and grander regarding the possibilities of life in a traditional sense. He thought he was doing, understanding, and teaching exceptional material as a physics teacher and as a minister. In comparison, where he is now, he feels his conceptualization was like a child in kindergarten. He's got a twinkle in his eye with amazement as to what he is experiencing on his new plane.

H: I don't want you to rush, or come before your time, but I want you to know … wait until you get here! Get ready, it's so mind-expanding, and we'll explore it all together.

K: I see you two sitting on a bench. You will be back together again. I'm feeling he's teasing you about how much you two share. It's reminiscent of the time when you were brother and sister in a past life.

H: Yes, that's how we were in that life. We'd explore. "Come and see what I found out." When you join me again, we will be able to discuss not only with each other, but also in groups here. Even in death, we explore thoughts and theories and we're able to express and share new concepts and ideas with others.

B: It sounds like he's having a good time.

K: Oh! He is!

B: Perhaps he remembers Arthur Ford, a medium, who got television airtime in the 60s or 70s about life on the other side. I wonder if that concurs with what Hal is finding.

K: I never heard of the guy, but he has. While on Earth, Hal would have been wary of these conversations. He had a very religious-based belief system.

B: Yes, I would say very traditional. I think I was the one to expand his thinking.

K: Am I getting this right? If Hal were here on Earth, mediumship would not be comfortable for him?

B: Yes, he would be uncomfortable. The same way with Edgar Cayce. I've always been such a devotee of Mr. Cayce's life and work. Hal knew I was a groupie.

K: Yes, Edgar Cayce was out there for him too. But, he could almost understand the concept of Edgar Cayce more than a medium talking to dead people. The ability of a person conversing with the dead freaked him out, even though he's communicating through a medium now! [*laughing*]

H: See how much my world has expanded! [*laughing*]

B: [*laughing*] I think that's called eating crow!

K: That's funny! And he said it very nicely and tactfully.

B: He's nothing but honest! Before we end I have another question. In the first session I suspected information was being passed between our spirit guides to give helpful tips. I wonder, does Hal know who my spirit guide is?

H: I know them all.

B: Hal, you should give both our spirit guides a big hug because we have given them such a big workout in this lifetime.

H: Yep! My guide's name is Stanley.

K: Beverly, I really do think that Bob might be your spirit guide. He's got amazing energy, a big smile, a nice sense of humor. Flippant sometimes, but very loving.

B: He might be. I have a quirky sense of humor too. When I think back, Hal was often asking deep, important questions. He always seemed so secure and comfortable with himself but I liked to tease. Sometimes I'd give him frivolous answers. I always had to joke away.

K: You know what? Bob could be your spirit guide, because he too has the same kind of personality. He's jovial, but there's a little bit of flippancy about him. Our spirit guides speak through us, so inevitably they let their personality be seen too.

B: Maybe I should have had a real sober kind of guide.

K: Oh no you don't! I have one of those. I'd pick the jovial one any day. Oh, oh! My guide, Timingo, is shaking his head, saying, "Oh, Kym, you really didn't say that, did you?"

Oh, Timingo, don't worry. I wouldn't give you up for nothing! Kiss, Kiss!

Any more questions?

B: No, and thank you so much, all of you.

Beverly's Personal Journey:

I didn't mention it during this session, but I still feel embarrassed about my conduct since my first reading in autumn. In the span of time between the November reading and my receiving the audio recording of the session, I disappointed myself. Hal asked me to give my grief to Jesus, but I was lost in my own hurt. Releasing my ball of grief so Hal's soul and its goodness could be released back into the Universe was sidestepped. I was wrapped up in personal insecurities. If I did this, I was afraid my friend would be taken from me again.

Nevertheless, I forced myself to find a ball into which I could symbolically place my grief. On a clear, crisp Sunday walk I found the perfect answer when I spotted an Osage orange tree which had begun shedding its wonderful, puffy, knobby, yellowish-green fruit the size of a big softball. I figured I would use this fruit to harness my grief and bury it. Hal and I had long ago agreed the wild Osage orange was one of nature's decorative delights. I scooped up a couple of fruit balls and walked home. Days passed, and I still hadn't found the right mindset to release my grief. I still hadn't processed the totality of the purpose of the exercise. My intellectual intention was when the ball of grief was buried, in time, it would take root and grow into a new tree to bring joy because its goodness had been released.

When I finally took one of the Osage orange balls to the edge of my property adjacent to the woods, I tried to dump all my grief into the round fruit, but I knew I was still angry and resentful. I couldn't release the grief.

I couldn't think beyond my own pain to focus on the greater benefit. I trudged back to the house in tears knowing I was dragging my grief back with me as I slammed the door shut. I wasn't ready to see, accept, and drop my viewpoint that the ceremony was all about my pain. Thus, I was forcefully stifling Hal's soul by not allowing him to be free of my spiritual immaturity. I interpreted the message as choking my friend with my selfishness. It didn't compute. I didn't realize I was not being asked to give up my friend, I was being asked to give up my grief.

I'm left with the guilt of clinging to the past until I can willingly rejoice, let go of my grief, and say, "Here world, I'm happy to share my friend's wonderful goodness!" Until then, no new little Osage orange tree, whose seed was filled with my anger, will sprout on the little slope near the woods. Unfortunately, when Hal said in the first reading that he would continue to help me through some rough spots ahead, I didn't have the wit to realize this was one of the spots, nor take the opportunity to say, "Hal, I regret my slowness. Thank you for your help then and now."

Kym's Professional Journey:

As we get into this next session, Hal offers up a few bits of information. He makes comments about how his and Beverly's lives were "planned down to the details." I have been lucky to have a comprehensive training by my guide, Timingo, on this topic. I believe it will help to understand this invisible structure better. Here's a simplified overview.

Timigo's Teaching:

Our soul is a fraction of a bigger soul, the God soul. In order for the God soul to experience all it has created, it asks the little soul fragment to go to Earth to experience a small part of this creation and report back. This little soul makes a choice of what it chooses to experience, called a *life theme*. The life theme has two sides. It can be the receiver of the life theme or the giver of the life theme, and both have value. For example, "rejection" is the life theme where you can be a person who rejects others (giver) or is a person who is rejected by others (receiver).

The little soul fragment works together with its true soul mate who is their spirit guide. They devise an outline which lays out all the details of the coming earthly trip: starting with what sex the little soul will be, including the physical appearance, the family into which the soul will be born, and all the possible events of the little soul's life. All decisions are based on one question: "What is the best choice for the soul to experience this life theme?" (example: rejection).

Examples of life themes are love, martyrdom, rejection, forgiveness, self-loathing, courage, dependence, independence, power, grief, orphan, etc.

In this outline, each and every experience, event, and person the little soul interacts with will allow the little soul to experience their life theme in varying ways and degrees. The little soul is the co-creator of this entire life event. In order to fully experience their life with this theme, they need to forget they have created it in order to have all the fun of experiencing it all in its wonderment.

Look for our book about *outlines* to be released in 2017.

Personal Growth Questions

1. Were you pleased to realize spirits read more than just your thoughts so that they get a fuller understanding of what's going on with you at any moment?
2. How does the idea of a detailed outline planned in advance for your life make you feel? Comforted, trapped, puzzled? What kind of a message were you sending to yourself with your life theme?
3. Have you noticed how eager crossed-over souls are to let you know they're aware of your current life? Have you had such inklings? If you haven't, does this chapter begin to open your mind to such possibilities?

Private Moments Are Not Really Private!

April 5, 2010, Beverly's Mindset

Once again, it's birthday time. This time it's Hal's big day, so I made an appointment with Kym to acknowledge my buddy officially.

I've continued to think through my stubborn resistance to releasing grief as described earlier. My stubbornness amazes me, but I'm beginning to comprehend the goal of dumping my grief in order to help Hal and I move forward on our life journeys, something which needs to be addressed.

The last few days I've found myself thinking about my health, both the highs and the lows. For example, when I recently finished a huge, three-year project of over forty historic draperies for the Taft Museum of Art, I was thrilled by the work and its results, but I was totally exhausted. I thought that after I reestablished a decent sleep pattern my body would repair itself. It didn't. In 2006, when I was confronted with a cancer diagnosis, I undertook a crash course in options available to me. Studying the choices and deciding for myself what treatments were compatible with my goals was refreshingly empowering.

The low of my lack of sleep and energy is still an issue. But I have to push these thoughts aside, after all it's Hal's birthday. It should be all about him.

Once again, my phone rings at the appointed hour and I don't hear my voice tremble when I say, "Hello, Kym. May we get started now?"

Beverly (B), Kym (K), and Hal (H)

K: Hal's sitting right here laughing at you, so let's get started.

H: I've been waiting. I like these dates.

B: [*chuckling*] That's nice, so do I. When I hear that you've arrived early for our appointments, obviously "Rev. Hal Never-on-time" must have turned over a new leaf! Maybe what you needed on Earth was the ability to be in two places at the same time!

But seriously, for me, these readings are the easiest way, because I have not been terribly successful keeping appointments with Hal. Of late I haven't been leading an orderly life, except for my morning sauna to detox. It's hard to concentrate on him when I'm sweating.

H: Yeah, you're right about the convenience of splitting up. I needed it on Earth! Even though I'm with you a lot, these readings build up anticipation in me to know you are totally focused on me.

B: Yeah, me too. When I walk down to the grocery store I enjoy letting my thoughts wander. Sometimes I feel Hal has joined me on these long hikes.

K: Yes, he does.

B: In our last conversation we talked about setting a regular contact time, but it's a struggle to figure out a time to do it. I'm sure he sees that I have a terrible sleep problem. Often I get so sleepy that I quit and go to bed, or I fall asleep in a chair. Either I'm asleep at seven-thirty PM and wake up at midnight for the rest of the night, or I don't fall asleep until midnight and wake up a few hours later.

K: He wants to address your sleep pattern. In the early evening hours, you seem to just pass out. I feel it's quickly—

bam, you're asleep. He says something else is going on with you. Let me ask what he means.

H: When she passes out, it's not a deep sleep. She doesn't feel rested. She has sleep apnea, but not the common type. Go to a doctor and get it checked, because her brain is not getting properly oxygenated.

B: Okay, I just went to the chiropractor. What does Hal think about that experience? Physically, I feel much better.

K: Yes, I can feel in my body that you've gotten realigned properly.

H: Yes, it was good, but this is something different. I want you to continue with the chiropractor because you keep slipping back out of alignment. It's a good practice for you to do, but other things are thrown off. You should talk to the chiropractor about your sleep issues. You'll be really surprised what the chiropractor can do.

K: I feel what you need is more than just a regular chiropractor. Is this a chiropractor who does homeopathy?

B: Yes.

H: Homeopathically, he can help with your sleep issues.

B: I wonder if this was part of my mother's problem. Poor lady had such a struggle with sleep. Does Hal have an opinion?

H: It would have helped her immensely. People don't think of chiropractors as being diverse, but they are. Your chiropractor is the first line of defense. Continue to get aligned, which balances you. Keep that up, but talk to him about other issues you wouldn't normally think to mention. The more he knows about you, the better he can help with his additional homeopathic knowledge. He does muscle testing to see what remedies your body will respond to best.

B: Yes, he found something for my digestion and a gum problem with the muscle testing. I remember in our former church membership there was one chiropractor and one surgeon. Professionally, there was great tension between them.

At the time, I was a bit wary about chiropractic since it was not part of my upbringing. Similarly, I had observed that Hal was also into Western medicine. Three decades later, when I contracted a serious disease and decided to treat it aggressively, I cranked up my courage and sought alternative options to Western medicine. That's when my eyes were opened to the benefits of other methodologies.

I have to chuckle. Hal's advice today is fully in the chiropractic camp, but how ironic we've both independently made a 180-degree turn in our health opinions!

H: Please, Beverly, do it quickly, because you're not getting sufficient oxygen to the brain. You can't just let this rest.

K: Maybe there is other stuff needing attention. For the chiropractor, did you fill out a long questionnaire about your life?

B: No, but I spent a lot of time telling him things I thought might be of importance to him. I have a nurse acquaintance who has practiced homeopathy for her family. She explained how important our attitudes are and how they affect our physical body in becoming sick and in our recovery options. Healers need to know a lot about the patient for successful treatment.

K: One of my clients is a homeopathic practitioner in Minnesota. To help me in Ohio, she sent me an unbelievably long questionnaire, maybe 25 pages long. The questions ranged from the dynamics of my family at my birth, to weather conditions where I live today. It shocked me to realize how much information she needed in order to tune into the background of my disease issues.

In your case Beverly, there's something in your thought process making you susceptible to sadness. Homeopathic remedies can help with depression and negative thoughts instead of the drugs a physician would prescribe. Hal says yours is not outright depression, but loneliness and sadness overflows you at times. Sleep apnea and loneliness are now believed to be connected.

Hal is showing me the scientific way. He's connecting atoms—this is attaching to that. Sadness and loneliness attract each other. They need to be dealt with in separate ways, yet in the end they can help each other. Beverly, I'm currently sitting in a hallway surrounded by beautiful, chocolate-brown curtains printed with circles. All of a sudden I see these circles on my curtains pop out and connect to each other like atoms. Hal's funny. He's using what's around me to give me a chemistry/physics lesson. He's always the teacher!

Hal predicts that you're going to feel tremendous in the warm weather.

B: Yes, plus a little vitamin D sunshine will help too.

K: You're going to have these things cleared up. Your sleep will improve, and you will be dealing better with your loneliness and sadness.

B: Looking forward to it. Hal has probably seen me watch the DVD called *The Living Matrix*, which covers a lot of energy topics. Is some of that on the right track? In fact, are these concepts trickling down from where Hal is?

H: A lot of it is very accurate. I am surprised people are able to get these concepts so soon in the current evolution. Everything on Earth is moving very quickly energetically. Humans weren't supposed to get some of these concepts for a while. However, they're coming into existence because people are getting to the level of enlightenment where they can take the information in and regurgitate it out into concepts laypeople can understand. It looks like chaos is going on, but it's not. The Earth has been pulled quickly into a higher vibration. It appears everything is falling apart, but really it's dislodging unneeded crap.

K: Hal's showing me a vision of a car from the movie *Back to the Future*. All things can't move to the higher vibration. As the car shoots through space, it loses parts which are excess weight.

Everything seems to be in chaos, but it's only unnecessary parts falling off. In the end, the car is functionally sleek and streamlined in its new destination. This vision symbolizes us moving to a higher evolution and dropping our baggage.

B: Will all of us be able to keep up? Being set in our ways is a problem. Desiring or accepting change is not always easy.

H: Yes, we will, but a lot of people will decide to check out. Their attitude is "I'm done." They choose not to stay any longer. Beverly, that's not you! Even though you're in your higher years, your mind of acceptance and wanting to learn is still there. You have the choice, just like anybody else. I see you as deciding to stay on. You're choosing to comprehend, implement, and move to the next level of enlightenment.

B: Yes, I do want to stay, but I still struggle. So much of my teetering between happy and sad reflects my current, rather isolated life. There are only so many people in my circle willing to talk in detail on the expansive topics I prefer, so I frequently find it a lonesome life.

K: They're showing me a film settling over you. Your sleep problem and the film is causing additional fogginess. Once you get that film off, your extreme openness and negative perceptions will dissipate. Then you can make some choices after you're clear. You'll be more interested in seeking out people because you have so much to offer. Do you go to library functions?

B: Yes, I do. I don't have a computer, so I mostly use the library's equipment for my business needs. For years I've participated in the local book club, but they prefer fiction. I like the stimulation of non-fiction, so my attendance has decreased.

K: I understand. Hal's saying it's the social part you need most. I'm sensing an already established group. There are easily three people you can connect with in that group. One's a man and the other two are women. I feel it's a book club with a common thread upon which relationships can be built. I think it's the man you attach to because you like having conversations with intelligent men. It's an element you need. Or, look around for another book club.

B: The local book club doesn't have any men … Oh! Hal's probably referencing the numerous church book studies. Yes, I always find them thought provoking. I'll check into it. As for men, I often feel more comfortable with them than with women. I recognize my tendency toward the male characteristics of one-track focus, independence, and physical skills, which all come so easily to me, so I can relate to men.

K: I'm naturally very attached to my male side also. My nurturing female side has been neglected, so for the last few years I have consciously started to work on that. I find balance is important in all things.

But Beverly, you need the male perspective. You need opportunities to find intelligent men. If you find a few extra, throw them my way! [*laughing*]

B: [*laughing*] Okay, they're all yours. I want to revisit our conversation of last month concerning the planning Hal and I did for our current life, when we would meet, and his departure in advance of me. What was the reason for that decision?

Parallel to those questions is, on the other side we planned for him to be thirteen years older than me, does that mean for thirteen earth years I sat and twiddled my thumbs waiting to be born? What was I doing? I can't imagine myself twiddling my thumbs! Was I his imaginary babyhood spirit friend? Or a spirit teacher kibitzing with his parents to be sure they were doing a good job? So what's your answer?

H: Oh! It feels good to hear all those popcorn questions of yours. You've never twiddled your thumbs anywhere! While I was being born 13 years prior to you, you went on to another life where you died rather quickly as a child with pneumonia. As that child you were a great gift to your father and mother. Even though your life was very short, it was very profound for many. You came in like a miracle, bringing them great gifts, but you left early. You wanted to experience being the miracle child.

B: The mechanics of organizing the who, what, when, where, and why of people's lives is mind boggling!

K: Isn't it! God is amazing in the details!

H: You're not wasting time on Earth now either. It seems you're sitting, waiting, but you're not. You still have events to experience and things to teach.

B: Is that my and Hal's purpose now? For me to be his mouthpiece?

H: You've never been anybody's mouthpiece!

K: He's laughing at your terms.

B: But I'm not a verbal person!

K: No, you're here to teach somebody something, I feel, in small groups of two or three people. It's important. You need to be in your teacher mode. You have gathered a lot of information in many different ways.

Hal's simplifying this for me. You had to meet him at this point, after his death, so he could teach you some concepts to share with this small, intimate group of people. It's your role for the remainder of this lifetime. Teach your ideas and what you know in your soft style. I don't feel you're necessarily in a classroom teaching this.

B: Is it more one-on-one, like a Cayce group?

K: I think it's bigger. It's time to disperse your knowledge, your ideas, and information in a variety of ways. You're the wise one who is left to teach the youth, as grandparent to a child. This is where you are right now. You need to be your own mouthpiece.

B: I'm the last person! I'm not capable.

H: You're completely capable. You saw me on a pedestal and needed to lean on me while you learned. You have all the concepts and knowledge you need, not just from me, but from life. Believe in yourself. It's your role now. It's your turn now to be the front man.

B: Yeah, teaching is all about answering questions. In a note to you, Kym, I mentioned how often you'd say to me, "Nobody ever asked me that question before." What the heck? Am I asking the wrong questions?

K: No! You're asking the right questions. You're a thinker. Most others don't think beyond their basic questions, "When will I meet Mr. Right? When will I make money? Should I quit my job?" You're on a much higher level than my typical client.

B: Do you like to work with people like that? Doesn't it drive you nuts?

K: Of course it does. But I have to work with clients where they are. Timingo teaches, "Always start with a person's existing thoughts and beliefs then help them grow into greater understandings from that point." People need to take a step at a time. Most people are incapable of making large leaps. Use baby steps, like Hal is doing with you here.

B: Oh, I get it. Hal's working with ministers who don't understand what their mission is. You work with clients on healing issues they have. For me, I don't know what my field of expertise is.

K: Beverly, your growth and your wisdom needs to get out in the world. Do it with writing because it spurs you on. Written word is teaching in itself. It forces the writer to analyze their viewpoint by going deeper into their own psyche. In that exercise, authors question themselves, then they share.

H: Don't die with your concepts and perspectives unspoken. Don't die with your thoughts and feelings still in you. To be fulfilled, what you wanted to do in this last part of your life was to teach. You are a teacher. Teach. What you question gets people to think.

K: Your expertise is asking questions. Just like you do with me in the readings, you ask me questions. Your puzzlement stretches me, you get me to think. As you talk with people and ask them questions, it allows others to stretch through your knowledge and wisdom. Any way, any shape you can do it, do it.

B: That's a lot to think about, but I promise I will later. My friend Hal and I often talked about philosophy and theology. In our discussions we bantered around a lot of theories, so now that he's on the other side, one of the things I am curious about is how many good guesses did we make?

H: Some right, some wrong, but proposing theories was important. It was good mental exercise. It piggybacks on the statement of how you teach through your questions. In our conversations, you may not have brought up new concepts; it was your questions that were new to me. You may not have known it, but you brought illuminating clarity to my old thought patterns. Bev, in your questions you let the person you're talking to open up and expand, like you did with me. It's what you do really well. Even when you're sharing your own ideas, it spurs on questions in others which expands them. That's your greatest gift.

When one only comes from a single viewpoint in his own head, he gets very one-sided perceptions.

Beverly, talking to you is like pop, pop, pop. I call that the Popcorn Theory. You get ideas and phrases, then you express them as questions, not complete concepts or thoughts. The depth of your questions spurs us on to the next level. That's your greatest gift. Even when you just share your life, it expands others. You're not pushing your thoughts on them. You're giving them things to think about. What you are doing is self-educating them. You only see it as, "Well, I don't know anything. I just asked questions." Your curiosity is your brightness. It's where you're brilliant. You ask very clear questions that just bam people in the face!

K: So many people are muddled. I have to say to my clients, "Just stop a moment and think!"

B: I go over and over things in order to get deeper or clearer understanding. Sometimes I feel like a stuck record.

K: What you're doing is part of your process; you look at every aspect. Hal's showing me a cow chewing her cud, the pokey way she pulverizes and digests her food.

B: [*chuckling*] Oh! I get his point. That's right on target!

H: Yes, your process can become tedious and slow, but that's part of your brilliance. However, too much of anything is not balanced. For you, the cud-chewing process works well in writing.

B: As to writing about personal spiritual values, I've always left that up to others. If Hal can give me some topics or concepts he wants to express, I'm open to taking dictation. Or, can he type them? I've got a typewriter here. Can he still type?

K: How about automatic writing? He's showing me you writing longhand. Do you like to write that way?

B: Yes, just as he did with a pen when he wrote his sermons. Actually we both preferred that method because ideas always seemed to flow directly from the brain through the arm and fingers to the pencil or pen.

K: He said he'd love to do automatic writing through you.

B: Really? Are you kidding? Well, there was a time when I did automatic handwriting, but after a while I thought foolishness started coming through, so I stopped. Now I could do it while I'm in the sauna where my relaxed brain is too limp to think actively. The warm air might even help.

H: I would love to do it if you're interested. I could easily learn to do it with you. Automatic handwriting would be good, because you'll have tangible communication in a method familiar to you for processing.

B: How would I know it was him?

H: Sit down, meditate a few minutes, breathe through your nose and out through your mouth, relax into a meditative state, and just wait for your pencil to write propelled by my energy. Thinking is not allowed by the receiver.

B: When I did it before, I didn't think about anything, my hand just moved. I put the pencil in my left hand because I'm right-handed. By writing from the opposite side of my body, the brain is less engaged in established habits.

K: You can do it with either hand. He says it doesn't matter. You'll know it's him. At first, it'll be stop and start. You'll question, "Is this me or him?" Then just allow the writing to come through. Don't worry about it, just allow it and be in the moment.

Hal talks to you all the time. He's here and wants to be part of this new experience. So why not? Write longhand. He loves that, you love that. Just do the method you both love.

B: I'll try to get him at a good time when he doesn't have other responsibilities.

H: I'll be there whenever you need me. Don't worry about that. You're not pulling me away from anything else. I could be in multiple places at the same time.

B: Oh, really? So he wasn't kidding. He can split himself up?

K: Oh yeah. I see him in lots of places. He can be with you and the ministers at the same time. Our earthly concept of being in only one place is not valid.

B: Is that true of everybody over there?

K: Yes, everybody. You're never an inconvenience to them, and you shouldn't think that you're a nuisance by making them stop things in order to be with you. Hal's laughing!

H: Beverly, you know, it's going to blow your mind over here!

K: We're here feeling so limited as humans. Yet when we go back home, we are so unlimited.

What an amazing gift God gave to us of forgetfulness. The gift is to forget we have superpowers.

B: Well, yeah. It's so annoying when you can't remember what you forgot!

K: Well, that's the process. If we knew, the game would be over. Any more questions?

B: There's always questions! [*laughing*]

K: We'll end this session here, but just think—you can talk to him through automatic handwriting. He's very excited about that. Also, he's happy you got the information about your health.

B: Thanks Hal, we'll talk again I'm sure.

Beverly's Personal Journey:

Where does the other side get such nutty notions as to think I can explain these subtle concepts? It's not like they're suggesting I brush off my art teacher skills to discuss the principles of design to a few folks. Yeah, my education and experience makes that logical, but why on earth were they buttering me up with flattery for something totally different from my schooling? It must be some kind of personal software glitch.

One idea really knocked me for a loop. A vital phase in my spiritual education was to take place with me on Earth and Hal on the other side. I knew back in the 70s that Hal as my tutor had a lot of wisdom to impart. Apparently his teacher role hasn't changed, only his location has. I have to hand it to him, he has described some surprising things in these sessions with Kym.

Another surprise of the reading concerns automatic handwriting. I don't feel really comfortable with that idea. As Edgar Cayce warned, you never know who's on the other end. To whom are you connected? Of the three of us, Kym, Hal, and me, I'm the only one who had a slight downside experience of automatic handwriting when I was in my thirties. Oh well, maybe I'm being too much of a worry wart. It should be a fun way to communicate directly.

Kym's Professional Journey:

In the last few chapters, Hal has access to additional skills on his level, by being with us whenever we need him by being able to split and be in different places at the same time. I had a client who was experiencing terrible grief for her father. She asked if her dad was also aware of his grandson's grief over his death. He said he was with his grandson all of the time because of that reason. She then cried and said, "Well Daddy, if you're always with him, what about me?" I couldn't help but laugh, because this was the first time a spirit told me about his ability to be with both the daughter and the grandson at the same time. We humans believe spirit is limited by our same human limitations, but Hal disproves that notion again here in this session.

I loved finding out that a crossed spirit is still able to continue to grow and change their minds, like Hal did with his new understanding about mediumship.

In my own journey through this book, much of my work is to see little pieces and parts, making some sort of sense of them. It feels like I've opened a puzzle box, but *without* the advantage of a picture to follow. As I put these pieces together, they bring up more questions, which I will share with you, our readers, for you might have some of the same questions.

My first question relates to the last chapter. With Timingo's teaching we were given a basic layout of the outline for the soul's *individual journey*, which is the starting point of the invisible structure. In this chapter, Hal talks about this same kind of outline. This time, not of the individual soul, but on a more global level, of *humanity's* outline.

Hal said, "Humans weren't supposed to get some of these concepts for a while. However, they're coming into existence because people are getting to the level of enlightenment where they can take the information in and regurgitate it out into concepts laypeople can understand."

So, if humans weren't supposed to know something yet, then there must also be some sort of written outline for humanity. If this is so, then are we as a human species able to make changes to this outline in a larger global way? It's outlined, but can it be changed? If we were not supposed to know yet, can our ability to move up the ladder of enlightenment change the *timing* for humanity to know things as a whole?

So, now we're aware that there is an individual soul outline in addition to a larger humanity outline. They all are a part of the invisible structure.

I once asked Timingo what spirituality and spiritual enlightenment really meant. He said the definition was, "Awareness equals enlightenment." He explained, "It's first awareness about self. As we learn about our own beliefs and motivations, we make choices for modification or forgiveness. We then grow. With our individual growth we become aware of other's beliefs and motivations and allow them the same choices of modification or forgiveness. All this awareness causes you to become more enlightened. The more you become aware about everything, the more enlightened you become. Simple."

Many times we on Earth have heard the quote by Richard Bach, "Like attracts like." Hal gives a lesson of how sadness and loneliness *attract* each other. This statement stuck out. To define it simply, yes, you have loneliness and it's logical you find yourself sad in your own pain of that loneliness. But I don't think this is all Hal is implying. I think it's more. *Sadness* has certain components to it that are the same as certain components in *loneliness*. It's those components which are energetically attracting to each other. We are given a similar teaching in a later chapter by a famous dead person, concerning another issue around the beliefs we hold and how they attract each other. But I wanted to bring your attention now to this first teaching on the subject.

Part of our individual outline includes the additional use of the influences of our past lives in this current life. Hal brings up an interesting past life of Bev's where she wanted to know how it felt to be a miracle child. In many ways it was a great past life to bring up. Many people feel the death of a child is a tragedy. The point of view of the soul *wanting the experience* of a short life puts a whole different spin on children or young people dying early.

Over the last few years, I have seen many TV shows and Facebook posts on young children dealing with life-threatening illnesses who are handling it in amazing ways. They are a gift to everyone around them. Mattie Stepanek, a young boy Oprah introduced in 2001, comes to mind.

Mattie was a little boy who was a poet and philosopher. His disease would cause him to have a short life, but the powerful effect the young boy had on the world—at least the Oprah world—was so powerful that 15 years later, he's my image of a miracle child. He went on to write books and speak in public forums until his illness came to deliver him back to his God-self.

Reader, take the time to understand that *we* wrote the outline of this life. We thought long and hard to devise this plan to experience a single life theme. The hows and whys of our lives should be seen as a well-orchestrated plan. Our life experiences were not done *to* us, but done *for* us *by* us.

Yes, I hear your shouts of disbelief and the long litany of examples followed by "Why would I do that to myself?!" I have been a part of the same choir myself. Once you determine the life theme you wanted to experience in this life, all those quandaries become evident. Finding out your life theme is imperative in order to understand and master your life.

Hindsight is wonderfully clear! Here in 2010, Hal is telling Beverly throughout the session that she needs to be teaching what she knows. He's telling us then that this book you're reading now will be coming into form, and we—we silly girls—didn't pick up that clue for years!

In this session, Hal suggests doing automatic handwriting with him, yet we had no idea of the consequences of that decision.

Personal Growth Questions:

1. Have you considered the importance of your mindset in preventing and improving physical health? Can you use your thought patterns as a helpful tool?
2. What portion of your understanding do you need to get rid of to become "sleek and streamlined" so you're in tune with the earth's movement into the higher vibrations of enlightenment?
3. Would balancing the male and female sides of your personality be beneficial?

Playing Detective

June 2, 2010, Beverly's Mindset

This is going to be tough. I've got to own up to a few facts. First, my intention to meet at a regular time with Hal has all but fizzled. Second, my efforts to connect with my spirit guide have been weak. Third, the automatic handwriting with Hal has been more successful, but all is not as it should be. Sometimes the messages I receive are factually incorrect and I detect disturbances coming from the other side about authorship. I'm doubting myself and feeling insecure. Have I worked my way back to having a good handle on my life? No, not at all!

It's been eight weeks since my last reading with Kym, but my world has completely turned upside down. I don't know how, why, or when the reins softly slipped out of my hands, but I was no longer directing the horse I was riding. By golly, I actually was doing what my riding instructor complained about forty years ago, "Your hands are too soft! You need direct communication with your horse through the gentle contact of the reins and bit. Otherwise, your horse is confused as to how and where you want to go." Yep, that's exactly how I am feeling, I'm not in control of my life. I relaxed, became inattentive, and now I am wondering where I am. I don't think I'm in charge anymore, though, with effort, I complete my daily obligations, but without peace of mind. I need a reading to help me figure out why I deteriorated recently to the point that my friends called the village police and I ended up spending the legally required three days in the mental hospital.

The telephone rings. I wonder how Kym will take my news. Maybe I better ease into my turmoil gradually.

Beverly (B), Kym (K), and Hal (H)

B: Hi, Kym, I'm happy to hear your voice again. Here's a good surprise. As I woke up early this morning, I think I had a conversation with Hal. Was he here? Was I hearing his questions and thoughts?

K: Hal's giving me a vision of himself sitting next to you. The way you're reacting, I thought you could hear him like two people having a chat. You're doing something with your hands. Do you knit?

B: Oh, I make my living sewing draperies for historic house museums. I'm not surprised he's with me when I sew.

K: You're sewing, and he's reading the newspaper. You don't look at each other, yet it appears you're talking with each other like an old married couple. I thought you could hear him now.

B: No, sometimes I can hear him when I'm doing automatic handwriting, but I've never heard him away from our written words before this morning.

K: Beverly, when we are in a reading, do you hear him? Sometimes I'm an amplifier and clients can hear better when I'm around. So, I'm just curious.

B: No, I don't hear Hal during your readings. I need to get his words from you.

K: Oh, okay. I'm curious about your technique on automatic writing. Can you explain?

B: To start automatic handwriting with Hal, I take a pencil in my non-dominant left hand and hold it softly in an upright position. Then I wait. With Hal, who's a beginner, usually the pencil shimmies in place gathering momentum until some force jolts it forward. The writing begins as I relax and let the pencil magically skim across the page. I have no idea what is about to be written.

At first Hal's letters were jerky, rough shapes slowly formed as he learned, from his perspective, a new skillset. With practice, he developed control of the size, shape, placement, and smooth flow of the words, just like I saw him do many times in life while writing his sermons and notes.

As for me, the other half of the team, I picked it up easily since I had done automatic handwriting decades earlier. However, I remembered well the days when receiving one word would laboriously fill a whole page!

Over the next few weeks as we progressed, I started to hear Hal's words as my pencil was being pushed to form the cursive writing. Soon the writing was small and legible as if it was done by my right hand. At that stage it was rather like taking dictation.

By May, I had a kind of "knowing" of what the next words would be, but I was still not controlling the pen, aside from cradling it upright. Eventually, I could go on correctly for a sentence or two without hearing a thing, then suddenly I'd go blank and stop in my tracks.

I could hear Hal—I guess it was Hal—say in an amazed voice, "How did you know what words were coming?" Telepathically, I said, "Honestly, I don't know how I did that nor why it stopped abruptly." This "knowing" experiment happened several times within multiple sessions. But it was not consistent.

K: Wow, that's true automatic handwriting. I converse with my guide, Timingo, and I call it automatic handwriting, but it's really dictation. I sit at my computer, I ask him a question. He talks in my ear, I write what he says. He's not pushing down the computer keys, it's me doing all the typing. I wish he would type it. He might spell better than me!

B: I want to ask some questions about my current concern over what has been happening to me. It's the reason for my scheduling this reading. I would like to have Hal's take on events.

H: I have been aware and concerned about what's going on. As happy and excited as I was about how clearly we were beginning to communicate, now I am worried. Other entities are coming in!

B: [*stunned*] Are we talking about my automatic writing?

H: Yes.

K: Hal's showing me that automatic handwriting has turned you into an open vessel or funnel. As an open vessel, information pours in from a variety of places. I see him talking and you're writing away what he sends. Then he sees you write things he didn't say. That's when he realized something was amiss.

B: Yes, some information made sense and other things began to feel false.

K: Yes, I see multiple energies coming into you, and Hal's concern growing. He tried to tell you that everything you wrote down didn't originate from him. You hesitated but quickly went on blissfully. I'm interpreting that Hal cannot see, hear, or sense other entities. The written words are what tipped him off.

Once a similar event happened to me where not all souls see each other. A deceased man showed up in a client's reading who was his sister-in-law but he wouldn't talk. Also, he wouldn't leave after the session. He just kept hanging out in my apartment. A day or two later I said, "Okay, Mister, what's going on?"

He showed great shame, sadness, and depression, and told me it was his fault his daughter died. His daughter, a crossed-over spirit, showed up. The problem was that the father couldn't see or hear her. Even though they were both dead, no direct communication was possible. At that moment I realized there must be more than one level of death.

Timingo told me to outstretch my arm. I did. I was surprised when the daughter, who was standing behind me, slipped her hand down through my arm and hand as if I was a glove she was putting on.

Next, I told her father to touch his fingers to mine. Bam. It was as if a heavy, dark curtain was yanked back allowing an intense light to flood into the room. Shock and surprise washed across the father's face, lighting up a bright smile as he saw his daughter once again! It appeared they needed a human to be the conduit between their two levels. After they talked, the daughter crossed her father over to the other side with her.

B: What a touching reunion for the two of them. I had no idea humans have the power to connect separated or lost spirits with each other. No doubt automatic handwriting is just one option to bridge the connection between the living and the dead.

I want to get back to the specifics of my case. So my writing alarmed Hal ...

K: Yes, he could read it. He said to himself, "No, no, what's going on?" He tried to override it. Your brief nauseated feeling was Hal's worry. He feels badly, because you started this automatic writing experiment because of his enthusiasm. He feels ownership of the situation.

B: True, I felt nauseated. I didn't know why.

But no, he shouldn't feel badly. I wanted very much to communicate with him. It's an ideal method, as you said, because the person can re-read the message. The problem was my fault. I didn't pray for protection.

K: Yes, overall you do need protection. He's giving me a vision of you sitting at a table writing with a funnel over your head. You and the funnel are inside a big white bubble, which is your protection. It's the protection that is shutting down who and what can come into your funnel.

B: Once while doing automatic handwriting with Hal in our relaxed, casual style with minor stops and starts, suddenly the writing style changed. Fast, steady, and confident, words just flowed out from an obviously accomplished writer of great skill. This form of communication was very comfortable for this author. Supposedly it was Jesus. I don't know how I got that sense. The idea blew me away!

Later another writer, who announced himself as Jesus, was definitely not the same entity. His writing style was clumsy, unskilled, and disorganized in thought. I only made a mental note of the contrast in skills. My alarm bells were a little muffled that day! In hindsight, I should have stopped the whole thing, realizing now it was an invading entity.

K: I'm asking Hal if it was Jesus talking with you or those playful entities messing with you. I can't believe these playful spirits were interacting with you at the same time as Jesus, if it was really Jesus, I mean.

B: Oh, no, you misunderstood, it wasn't at the same time. But they'd be fools if they were.

K: I don't think he could see any of them to verify if it was Jesus or not. I have a sense Hal's on a very different level. Timingo is showing me a picture of energy going into you and words coming out your hand.

B: Kym, can you detect if it's good energy or bad energy?

K: Well, I don't feel icky around the energy. A mischievous, unevolved soul is messing with you like a boy around sixteen or seventeen years of age. Teenage behavior doesn't understand consequences. Even on that side, they discover new powers and congratulate themselves, "WOW, I can say things to this lady and she hears. How cool! I'm just going to mess with her." I don't feel evil or negative energy, only young and unevolved.

B: An old memory, back over thirty five years ago, just popped into my head. I might have a sense of who the youngster is. The very first day I worked at the church with Hal, I learned one neighborhood kid was a terror. I never met him, but I saw him cut through the church parking lot on his bicycle. Hal warned me that the kid was a troublemaker. The next morning

I was told the boy had died tragically in an accident. The embarrassment was that the church people living nearby were secretly relieved he died. If this is the youngster, why would this kid be so hateful toward me? We never met! What's my connection? To get at Hal? Hal, does that ring any bells?

K: I actually feel a tall, lanky kid wearing a black outfit. Confused. Not truly mean-spirited. I'm asking if this is the same teenager who died so long ago. I'm asking Timingo, "Is there an attachment to Hal?" [*pause*] I think you're right. He is attached to Hal.

B: Well, Hal needs to be aware his family could be a target.

K: Yes, but if Hal's family is not in tune with the spirit world enough to feel the boy, no doubt he would seek someone else who was.

B: Oh, by doing automatic handwriting, am I more sensitive?

K: Yes, you are. *Normies* are people who are not sensitive to the spiritual side. A ghost or entity can't … Oh! That's what it is! The guy is a ghost! That's why Hal can't see him!

B: Oh, it's the kid who's a ghost?

K: Yes, he's the one lingering around you.

B: Well, can we do something to help him? Do we pray, "God, take care of him?" Is it the appropriate thing for this kid, or should we just leave it alone and mind our own business? The kid is causing me so much distress, I want this to be the last time I think of him. I want to proceed with my life.

K: Oh! Hal can't see him. The kid's still earthbound. No wonder they're not connecting. If he's a ghost, he needs help, and Hal is a familiar resource for him.

B: Certainly familiar! Their paths did cross. Hal was the only one in the neighborhood who stood up to the kid when he got into mischief. Now, all these decades later, this same teenager is pestering me while Hal and I are reestablishing our friendship through automatic handwriting.

B: You need to know, Kym, less than a month ago I was taken to the emergency ward late one evening. As I rested on the gurney waiting to be admitted into the hospital, control of my right hand was abruptly taken over. Violently, my hand was invisibly grabbed and flew across the bed sheet with the writing of my forefinger rumpling up the bedding.

Embarrassed and hoping no one had noticed, I began to smooth out the sheet. Lo and behold, I could actually see "Hal hates me" scribbled out by the wrinkles in the sheet. I was alarmed at the force of this energy and terrified of the anger in the terrible message of hate. I have no feelings like this toward Hal. I knew I wasn't the source of those words! In fact, Hal's lifetime motto was "I'm a lover not a hater." He unabashedly lived his motto.

I'll be darned. Now I get it! The message was from that teenager. Knowing I could do automatic handwriting, it makes perfect sense he was the author.

K: Wait! What? You were in the hospital? You didn't call me and let me know this! Beverly, why did you not call me if you were having such severe issues? This is very upsetting, I could have helped you!

Oh, I'm getting a chill.

[*annoyed*] Yes, Hal, the kid is still very confused and angry.

H: Oh, I know who it is! Let's see, what was his name? [*pause*] Tim!

K: [*to Beverly*] We'll talk about this later. I'm not going to let you off the hook on this hospital issue. Let's just deal with Hal. Together, we connected all those dots for Hal. Now he can concentrate on Tim, so he can sense him. Remember your earliest session Beverly, when Hal said he could actually watch a TV show if he focused on it? This is the same principle. How interesting! See, you're teaching Hal something!

While dealing with his own anger and frustration, this boy had unfinished business with Hal. In his desperation, Tim hunted down anyone who could get him to Hal. Since you were in communication with Hal, the kid used you.

B: Does Hal have a sense this kid was overseeing others coming into my writing? Or is he the only one? I felt other people coming aboard. I should have paid attention to those inklings.

K: What I'm learning is ghosts attract ghosts. Ghosts, being sociable humans, congregate. For example, a few months back, a young ghost girl who was murdered showed up to ask me to find her body. She brought with her a bunch of other ghosts. I was overwhelmed and said, "Wait! I can't handle all this needy energy at once. You have to leave my apartment, stand in the hall, and wait your turn!" Over the next week, I worked one-on-one with them to cross over.

So Tim must have put out some energy, on the ghost level, to say, "I'm going to talk to a sensitive." Other ghosts hearing this just showed up looking for assistance too.

B: Absolutely. In addition, these ghosts are awful good at imitating Hal. I wrote some of their nonsense, which is now polluting my mind. Which notions are true? Which ideas are to bamboozle me? I'm left to sort out those messages and decide what's real. My dilemma is compounded by my knee-jerk reaction that any voice in my head is directly from God. Where that idea came from, I don't know. Originally, these pesky statements came with my automatic handwriting, but now words are starting to enter directly into my head, which means they are randomly beginning to infiltrate my daily life beyond the moments I spend in automatic handwriting. Such access is a step in the wrong direction.

Back in the 1970s when I first tried automatic handwriting, some wonderful messages came through. However, I soon backed away from the writing when I connected with a foolish correspondent. Currently, these entities are decidedly nastier than those in the 70s.

This reminds me of a friend I had years ago from whom I eventually distanced myself. She drifted heavily into what I considered fringe psychic phenomenon entertainment—like séances, Ouija boards, and Tarot cards—which I wasn't into, since I was on a more religiously spiritual path.

In the teachings of Edgar Cayce, I was cautioned about such focusing tools. He said it wasn't the tool as much as who was manipulating it from the other side. I wanted to keep control of myself. Even as a toddler my mantra was, "I'm the boss of me!" In summary, at this juncture I don't know what to think of automatic handwriting in general and with me specifically.

K: Cayce was right; spirits can have their own agendas.

B: The other day, I was coming to the conclusion they wanted to kill me.

K: I don't think they are out to hurt you necessarily. Tim was trying to convince you to help him. He felt you pulling away from automatic handwriting because of all your other disturbances. He panicked. He didn't want to lose his chance to connect with Hal. On the bright side with automatic handwriting, you and Hal were communicating. It was fulfilling the more you developed your skills, but you needed protection to reach only those whom you desired without becoming an open receptacle.

B: So, is Hal suggesting I continue writing?

K: Yes.

B: Easy for him to say. But how? I don't think you're identifying with my position. I'm not being visited by an occasional courteous, polite voice with helpful hints from Heloise. No, I'm starting to get overwhelmed by a rabid multitude of conflicting distractions that shake me up. Saying to them, "Back off a minute and let me think through what you're telling me," is fruitless. This uncontrolled incivility is starting to scare me!

K: Remember, protection and intention are very powerful in and of themselves. Your goal is to talk only to Hal and protect yourself from these lower energies who just want to rattle people like you.

B: Granted, I was too informal. I just plopped down and said, "Okay Uncle Hal, what have you got to say?" Such was the extent of my prayer or preparation! A mistake I naively made was to think he and I were on a private telephone line. Wrong! Like it was in the 1960s when I first lived out on the farm, people had either a four- or eight-household party line for their phone service. As you can imagine, everybody could, and did, listen in on all the neighbors' conversations. Today I failed to realize I was still on a party line, but these voices didn't have human bodies!

K: I don't know if you need to be traditional in your protection setup. Do whatever is required to focus. If you need to say a prayer, say a prayer. If you need to light a candle, do it. Center your thoughts to say, "I want to deal with my guides and the highest energy available to protect me so I can talk to Hal."

Beverly, our session is coming to an end. Do you have a better handle on your current concerns now that you and Hal have a greater understanding of who the troublesome boy is? As for your hospital visit, Beverly you need to let me help you. If you find yourself in trouble, you have to call me. Day or night, I'll be there. We'll come back to talk later, but are you okay for now?

B: Yes, taking a break will give me time to piece together what just happened.

K: Hal, what do you suggest we do with Tim? Can you help him at this stage?

H: Now that I can sense him, I'll take care of the boy.

Beverly's Personal Journey:

I'm impressed. Each of us contributed information from our own side, thus we were able to put together what we knew about Tim to figure out the complex rescue of one lost teenage boy.

Actually, the whole conversation went better than I feared, but it's true I should have kept Kym in the loop. By getting overwhelmed so gradually, I didn't notice the downward trajectory of my mood until suddenly one evening a switch was flipped in my head with a voice announcing that I was slated to die immediately. It wasn't true, but I was so frazzled I believed it.

The timing was critical because simultaneously my guide deliberately urged me to push through the troublesome voices in order to regain my psychic aptitude using an old familiar ability, automatic handwriting. I observed the persistent encouragement by my team to keep trying to break through the layer of obstructions, to focus on my intended communicator, and develop clairaudience. Unfortunately, I allowed my eagerness for communication with Hal to overrule my vigilance and plunged ahead recklessly. However, my point here is a cautionary tale. Do not go into automatic handwriting lightly. It's not a play toy. I serve as an example of what can—and does—go wrong.

Kym's Professional Journey:

In this session, we are starting to realize Beverly is psychic, but in a different way than I am. Psychic ability is an innate human skill, and it had not shown up in Beverly's life consciously until she opened herself to automatic writing. With the additional factors of her deep grief, which weakened her emotionally, it made this psychic opening more traumatic. My concern for her well-being is starting to grow.

In this session we are getting clear information about some of the voices Beverly is encountering. Some involve ghosts. As part of the invisible structure, ghosts play an important part of the evolution of the soul. For a myriad of reasons [*which we delve into more later in this book series*], not all of the deceased go directly into the light.

With the arrival of this teen spirit, we are given some juicy nibbles of insight into another level of existence in the ghost level. Just like a crossed spirit, a ghost still keeps their personality and mode of operation, in Tim's case, annoying, bothersome teenage behavior. He was a bit of a hellion in life and he was still that same way as a ghost.

Ghosts:

- They have the same personality and behaviors as in life.
- They can interfere with humans who are sensitive to them.
- Their feelings are amped up and intensified. If desperate in life, they are off-the-wall desperate in death.
- As in this case, some don't seem to understand or care that their needs can cause so much chaos in a human's life.
- They can do automatic handwriting. Tim could control the hand of Bev, on the bed sheets, even when she wasn't in an automatic writing session.
- Not unlike some of the living, they feel they are trapped by their circumstances.
- They can seek out humans to help them.

Crossed spirits, being on a different level, can't see ghosts unless they become aware of them. To become aware, they must turn their focus on them, at least on the level of existence that Hal is on. [*We find out later that crossed spirits on higher levels can see ghosts.*]

In the first chapter Hal told us he was working with ministers here on Earth, as a spirit to human connection. But something came up in this session that is making me sit up and take notice. Both the crossed spirits and ghosts need the human connection in order to connect with each other. Here, Hal couldn't see Tim until he was told by Beverly that Tim was in attendance. That insight triggered my story about the way I connected a ghost father and his crossed spirit daughter through my hand. So I'm starting to think that the live human connection is somehow more of an integral part of a connection between the other levels of the invisible structure than I first thought. Do they need us as much as we need them? Is this a two-way street of helping each other evolve?

[*What do you think reader?*]

The process of communicating with spirits is varied. They each have different pros and cons, as Beverly is quickly becoming aware of.

As we progress through the session, Beverly is telling us how her psychic abilities are developing. Here she's easily able to talk to crossed spirits, Hal and this Jesus fellow. The interaction was easy and flowed well. Then, although it was choppy, she was picking up the words of ghosts, Tim and this false Jesus guy. So she could easily channel higher beings, but she was a bit more clumsy in getting the words from lower energies from the ghost level. Beverly also told us that she could sense the difference in their skillset from one spirit to the next by the writing which they were able to transmit to her, whether it was done easily or in stops and starts.

More psychic development was spotted when I described a teen energy that was bothering her. She got a "knowing" that it was this teen from about thirty-five years back. That is a psychic hit if I ever saw one! She didn't even realize the clarity of that hit. I found it particularly interesting that in the 70s Beverly was doing automatic handwriting naturally and only stopped because she became annoyed at some silly replies.

What if she hadn't stopped back then? What if she continued to refine the skill and thus her psychic abilities? Why are we being stopped from developing that skill further? Why do we get so scared? Is it the unknown element? Is it the out-of-control feeling that lets the fear take over?

First, I want to clarify here, ALL PEOPLE ARE PSYCHIC. Everyone enters this life with this ability. To what degree is based on our openness to it and our interest in developing it. In teaching, I see people who have locked down their abilities because they've gotten frightened. They either dismiss the experience as a coincidence or a fluke. They don't understand it, so they say it didn't happen, or they put it in some dark drawer in the back of the closet never to be opened again. Just because you don't see it doesn't mean it's not there.

Fear is the number one killer of your natural abilities. Many people have seen their recently departed loved ones sitting at the kitchen table and they say that it's their grief that "created this illusion." Yet deep down they don't even believe their own lie. If they do believe their experience and tell another family member, then they are told, "It's just your own mind playing tricks on you," or "Maybe you need to see a doctor." There's no quicker way to get someone to shut down their psychic abilities than by implying they might be crazy.

Many a highly psychic person can be found in mental hospitals, as Beverly is soon to find out.

Personal Growth Questions:

1. "At that moment I realized there must be more than one level of death." Have you ever thought about different levels of existence?
2. What thoughts were triggered by the introduction of Tim, the ghost seeking Hal? Did it scare you, titillate you, relax you, touch you emotionally?
3. Do you see why those of us here on Earth need to work together with crossed-over souls to solve our problems?

Facing a Big Bump in the Road

June 5, 2010, Beverly's Mindset

From the beginning, all my readings are full of encouragement for me to keep my energy and hopes up high whenever I try to communicate with my spirit guide through automatic handwriting. I start off optimistically, however I'm not successful. I can't seem to block out increasingly mischievous entities. Discouraged and depressed, I'm short on endurance. Maybe Kym will have some suggestions to offer me.

Similarly discouraging is the idea of developing secret identifying codes (like a tap or tingle) between my guide and me. It's laughable because I feel like I'm actually a fish in a glass bowl trying to find a hidden space under a rock to exchange a secret identifying word or tap. With each attempt I regularly give up in helpless frustration. My only fallback position is to schedule a date with Kym for a spirit guide session. So, once again I reach for the phone for a call from Cleveland.

Beverly (B) and Kym (K)

K: Hi, Beverly. How's it going for you today? Got any special questions or concerns?

B: I'm still trying to do automatic handwriting with my friend Hal and my spirit guide, but I'm struggling. Interference frequently upsets me with mean, negative, and false statements.

K: Is this abusive behavior only coming during automatic writing sessions, or are you experiencing it at other times?

B: Both in and out of the sessions. For example, just before my hospital trip when I thought I was dying, these spirits knew just the right buttons to push when I was feeling unloved and abandoned. I believe these are issues I brought with me into this life since my current family has always been a loving, supportive unit.

At the oddest times voices came to me, pretending to be other people. The tipping point came when—I believe—a fake Jesus declared I had committed an unpardonable sin because I sent compassionate, blessing thoughts to a friend who was going through a tough time. Outraged, the voice proclaimed, "How dare you! Only God is allowed to bless." The voice said death for me was imminent. Being doomed forever was my punishment.

Frankly, part of me wanted to chuckle. I was amazingly calm about the dying part, but I was upset with the concept of "forever." Something struck a chord with me. Processing this "Jesus" proclamation, I watched the back of my hands. When you are old, your veins stick out as the skin becomes as thin as tissue paper. But after my condemnation was announced, my veins became as narrow as silk threads. Where did all my blood go? My breath became shallow and difficult. Again, I thought it was verification that I was dying. These constant voices really scared me. It's the reason why I'm not feeling charitable toward the mischievous voices now especially since in my latest biofeedback session, it reported I'd suffered a tiny stroke.

If these voices started out as a prank, they had gotten out of hand. I blamed myself because I wondered... was it outsiders? Was it my subconscious? Was it the regurgitation of a past life belief system, a medieval concept of God? I was struggling with a lot of different spirits, but I was also evaluating and regretting stuff about myself in this life.

K: I'm so sorry you're having such a difficult time. Remember when we talked in our last session, your friend Hal spoke of you being too open? The most important parts are the protection you put around yourself and dealing only with the highest of energies. You're not alone. Your guides are with you.

When you said medieval, it jumped out at me. I think you're really on to something. Many of our past lives had unfinished business that we carried forward into this life to experience again. When real or imaginary feelings such as abandonment and insufficient love are triggered it can be an opportunity to clear up old stuff. As you talked, I got a vision. I saw layers of buttons piled on you from lifetime after lifetime. I think ghosts or unevolved spirits are good at finding and using these hot buttons, these weak spots, against you.

B: Absolutely.

K: And I think it's exactly what they did. They apparently knew you have a religious background. Jesus is a loaded symbol for many of us who had formal religious education, but you and I now have a broader spiritual base. We once believed in the hell of suffering punishment that has been taught for many lifetimes. Old, ingrained teachings are tender spots that get a reaction out of us. When we stop to think, we realize we don't believe most of these concepts anymore. So they should no longer be triggers for us, but old habits pop to the surface.

B: Was it part of my plan to experience voices in this life?

K: Yes, apparently you have done this before. You have channeled entities in a past life. This current situation is almost a repeat of a past life with your loss of power. Didn't I say you had some more work to do? In this life, once again, you have chosen to pull away from your own power. This is part of that work—remembering the power you have.

B: I know I have avoided stressful situations.

K: Your natural ability at automatic writing is an example of how powerful you are. These scary events of being harassed by voices are to help you to take notice. Didn't it make you feel really good to have this power of communication again with Hal?

B: Oh yes, it was good! Funny, I never doubted we could connect.

K: Yes, Timingo is telling me you had these same powers in other lifetimes. It apparently didn't always go well, so you denounced them. Already, early in this lifetime at the age of thirty-five, you relinquished this automatic handwriting skill at the first hint of trouble.

B: Yes, I dropped that early automatic handwriting as a waste of time when it turned into nonsense. Meanwhile, my physical Earth life was calling me to reach other goals instead. Knowing what I know now, I should have made a choice, back then, to deal with the troubled voice and push onward to reconnect with the wise voice instead. If I had gotten into difficulty and had an inability to cope with voices while pursuing automatic handwriting, I had several spiritually minded friends, Hal being one of them, who would have served as a support base.

Now here I am, over three decades later, dealing with, not one voice, but a barrage of negative voices that frighten me. They drain me. Yes, I'm afraid. Why shouldn't I be?

K: Well, that's understandable, but you were able to communicate with Hal and it was fulfilling. With the appearance of the unwanted voices, it means you have to work through your fears to talk only to those you desire. Learn to focus. Don't be an open vessel.

B: So they're saying I should continue writing?

K: Yes. When you sit down, make an intention. Ask for protection during each session so that your guides come in. Ask for angels to come and keep out anything that is not Hal and your guides. You need to say, "I only want to deal with my guides and the highest energy I can, so I'm able to talk with Hal." They say darkness is always chasing light. I don't like to describe it as a negative energy, but not all energy is in alignment with the power of light. You allowed fear to take you over. Instead of firming yourself up, you fell apart into fear. Thus, you stopped your own power and stopped doing the work.

B: Do I need to reclaim this power?

K: Yes.

B: I don't know why I keep asking you the same question, because I know the answer is yes. I'll work on this power issue later. Let me veer off again. The newest biofeedback programs can detect if a spirit is attached to you. My scans frequently registered an attachment. Thinking it is Hal, I usually tell Gloria, my biofeedback lady, to leave it alone. But maybe it's ghosts hanging around me. Do you have any insight? Is it Hal?

K: To tell you the truth, it's your spirit guide.

B: Bob, the tall guy at my birthday reading? Gloria forgets and zaps the attachment almost every time before I know it has appeared on her screen. Not knowing what it is, I haven't always objected. When I was discharged from the hospital, she put me and my house on the biofeedback program to zap both, and I felt much better.

K: Your spirit guide feels that's fine. If she zaps, it doesn't affect your guide like it would a spirit who has lower energy. Your spirit guide says he just needs to pull back a bit to not show up on the screen. He doesn't leave you.

B: So it's my spirit guide! I keep forgetting I have one!

K: Your guide wants you to spend time talking to him. You're moving Hal into the role of your main teacher.

B: Yes, you're right. I am.

K: Hal is on his own journey. He's not in the high level where your guide is. Your guide is not saying you shouldn't talk to Hal. He needs you to find time to talk to him, too.

B: Yes, I don't because I don't recognize him. Is his name Bob? Remember he was the flippant guy who observed us in the second reading?

K: I'm not sure, I'm hearing a really weird name that sounds more like Cherub.

B: I know a Cherith …

K: It's something like that. He's awfully tall to be called Cherub! [*laughing*] He's a very high level guide.

B: Does he want me to do handwriting with him?

K: Yes.

B: Oh my gosh! How do I close the funnel down?

K: Just ask. We all have different levels of energy we can work with in conversations. With Cherith, a higher level guide, you can make an intent to have a separate meeting. Say, "I want to speak to Cherith, and I would like the highest energies to assist in helping us communicate." Your guide oversees everything you do. He wants you to come into your power by giving you a lot of insight into your unfinished business. I'm asking Cherith what is the priority.

He says, "I want to connect with Beverly directly."

B: And my friend Gloria says that if I do this automatic writing again she'll absolutely strangle me! [*laughing*]

K: Of course. I understand her concern, but you have to work through your fear.

B: I know I have negativity attached to me. I have just sunk into a pattern of negative thinking.

K: It's because you have been avoiding your own inner power. In fear and avoidance of your own power, other entities can get to you in your weakened state.

I am very powerful. I have learned to control it and work it. I keep myself very clean by analyzing my motives and reactions to my experiences. When I do fall into fear, it makes me weak, and then I'm overloaded by spirits needing my attention. To stay in my own power is not always easy to do.

Protect yourself by not falling into fear. Grow further by vigorously engaging in activities you love. Stay in a positive frame of mind. Know who you are and why you do what you do. Self-analysis is the best work you can do for yourself.

B: Yes, use it or lose it.

K: Right, that's the problem. Are you going to repeat another life of trying to come into your power again? Wouldn't it be good to succeed in this lifetime rather than repeat it?

B: Definitely!

K: Reclaim your individual power with your guide.

B: Do I keep checking with you to verify who I'm talking to? Already two months have passed since Hal became concerned about other entities.

K: Yes, if you'd like. Consistently protect yourself every time before you communicate with spirits. Look at your recent experience as an extreme lesson that ended up with you in the hospital.

Early in my training, I was not listening about protection either. Timingo let people jump in and out of my body to scare the crap out of me. His point was to drum it into my head that I was not protecting myself. I needed the lesson. Timingo could have lectured me, "Kym, you are too open. People can jump in." Would I have heard him? I guess not, since he let me have a dramatic experience to store in my memory bank.

I think your frustrating automatic handwriting episodes served the same purpose. Unfortunately, instead of toughening yourself up, you freaked out and shut yourself down. You've already put down your powers and light for too many lives.

B: Five lifetimes ago?

K: Yes, I feel it started five lifetimes ago when you were really a powerful sorceress. Something drastic happened involving the sorceress. She shut her power down. Thus, in this power aspect, your soul is not growing.

B: No, my growth needs to be for the benefit of others. Whoops! That comment was not very self-loving!

K: No, it was not. In your life at this stage and time, you have to focus on yourself first. Others need to come second.

B: Yes, it's my time to reflect and work on this life.

K: We women of the recent century have difficulty with the idea of caring for ourselves first.

I too only accepted my power because I wanted to help other people. Like you, self-love is an issue for me. I will do things for others before I'll do them for myself. I eventually got it. Now I learn my lessons for my own growth first. After I've learned for myself, and only if I choose, I can help others with those lessons, but it's not my motivation any longer.

The guides are telling you this time period is now all about you, your growth and your connection to Source. They don't want you to worry about others, only you and Source.

B: Are the guides going to inform me of what I need to know?

K: Yes, your spirit guide doesn't want you to depend on Hal for telling you everything. You're not going to the highest source with Hal. You need to go to your guide. He will work with you.

Your spirit guide will give you a directive as to what to do. But it will always be in a positive way. If you start to feel anything in a negative sense, you need to stop the automatic writing, center, clear yourself, and make the intent to talk only to your guide. He wants you to sense him. He's going to send you a "knowing" of the way he feels, even though you're communicating through your handwriting. You will feel him. You will know you are connected to him.

B: Okay.

K: Hal can talk to you too, but he wants you to talk to your guide first so the connection to your guide will be stronger.

B: How about when we are done with our talk now, my spirit guide and I have a short session?

K: Yes, he's happy with that.

B: I won't tell my friend Gloria! [*giggling*]

K: You know your guide's only talking to you through your hand, but you want to develop trust. He wants to talk to you in your head like my two guides do with me.

B: So you can tell by their voices?

K: Not so much by the voice, but how they feel. Their energy is very different. My main guide is Timingo, who's at a lower level than Tobias. When Tobias shows up, Timingo just observes while Tobias works with me. Timingo is not subservient, but he's not on the same level as Tobias. Temporarily, I move up to the level where Tobias and I can talk together.

B: Maybe my spirit guide will write out his name?

K: Also, ask him to make you feel him, so you know it's him.

B: How do you feel your guide? In your whole body?

K: When I started with Timingo through automatic handwriting, he made my eye flicker, which I knew I couldn't control. I wasn't concerned about others popping in. Maybe I was naive. I can't read my own handwriting, so I used a computer. I just typed out a question and he'd give me an answer. We started communicating this way for a few months, then he felt I was ready to start feeling his presence more. I could sense his love for me. It was powerful!

B: To hear a voice would be much more comforting than writing.

K: Don't worry, you'll get there. It's a process. Do some automatic handwriting because you need something to read. Tell him what you want. You are the question girl, ask him questions! "What can I do to know it's you?"

K: Now I no longer need automatic writing to talk to Timingo. He talks through my head. I built up my trust. I don't always hear his voice, but I know it's him. Also, I know I have assistance from multiple guides.

Oh! Hal just popped in smiling happily. He was concerned because you kept sliding into the fear mode lately with all these other spirits popping in. Hal's showing respect to your guide by urging you to go to the guide for all the questions you have been asking him. He insists he doesn't want to lose connection with you.

B: Hal, I'll do as you suggest, I promise to talk to my guide.

K: He's saying you wrote this whole hospital experience into your plan before you came to Earth. You needed to be shocked!

B: I sure was! Well, I need to stop now to catch my breath. Thanks for helping me think through these events.

Beverly's Personal Journey:

This is a tough reading. How do I process this session? Parsing clear, useable information to analyze and implement in my life is a problem. The reading, upon reflection, is hopelessly filled with double talk.

My current main problem, I'm told, is discernment of who's talking to me in my head. I am to sense who is talking to me and adjust accordingly. If the talk becomes negative, I'm to disconnect and disengage, also known as fleeing, for which I have been scolded since my major withdrawal beginning five lifetimes ago through to this present life. Instead, I am to remain true to my own beliefs and not waver in my opinions. Frustrating! I can't win for losing!

What sensory tools have I at hand to assist me in my discernment efforts? I currently can't see, taste, or smell who is approaching me. When I am being strongly accosted, I feel tiny pin pricks, so perhaps touch is a warning. Of the five senses, hearing is the one that operates for me. I recognize and associate certain words or phrases with specific people, but that alone can be imitated. More importantly are the qualities of the voice, but frankly, with rare exceptions, the voices all sound alike in my head.

What other senses are there to tap into? Perhaps vibration, but I don't consciously feel anyone around me. Maybe my success will eventually come when I learn to attune myself to subtle vibrations, perhaps it's ultimately about reading energy as a sixth sense.

In the meantime, I struggle. Yes, I agree my willingness to be open causes me problems, because I often lack the background knowledge to make wise decisions. Likewise, my propensity to fall into fear gets me scolded too. Don't they know I don't want to be afraid? I assume fears are based on past experiences, yet figuring out how to bypass that emotion has so far escaped me. Honestly, this reading only makes me more frustrated since I don't see much practical guidance at this stage except for automatic handwriting. I don't particularly feel protection, but I'll carry on. The thought of going through another lifetime working on this same issue truly makes me break out into a cold sweat!

Kym's Professional Journey:

As the session progresses I am getting more and more concerned with what Beverly is sharing. The fact that she is dealing with an onslaught of negative voices, which are not only affecting her in her automatic writing sessions but also throughout the day, is a red flag for me.

This wasn't the first time I have come up against someone being hijacked by their psychic abilities. I had an on-again, off-again relationship with a young girl, Ellie, who was seeing ghosts and hearing voices at around the age of eight. Her mother was a coworker of mine at a flower shop and I had just come out at work that I was a psychic. My friend enlisted my help for her daughter. Being pretty new at this work myself, I didn't know what to do aside from just talking with the child.

Her psychic awakening began when Ellie was awoken with an old woman ghost looking at her as she napped on the couch. Ellie, of course, was startled, but for some reason she didn't feel afraid. The old woman said that she needed Ellie to talk to her daughter who lived in the apartment below. The grandmother had a warning concerning her daughter's teenage son.

Ellie was not at all comfortable with delivering such a message. Plus, there was always a lot of commotion coming from that apartment, so Ellie was wary. I really didn't know how to help Ellie at the time, but I reassured her that I believed her. To empower Ellie, I told her she could just tell the woman she couldn't do as she was asked. A few days later, the elderly woman came back and Ellie followed my advice. The woman disappeared and never returned.

Ellie was having a very difficult preteen and teen life, and got involved in troubling situations. I no longer worked with her mom, so I didn't know of many of the struggles that followed this young girl. It wasn't until she was about 25 years old that she located me again. By this time her life had gotten quite small. She had many visits to mental wards, therapy, and medications, all thanks to her seeing spirits. She was constantly accosted by spirits in her home and unable to keep a job due to anxiety over what *might* happen. Further triggering her anxiety, being a new mom, she had concerns over the safety of her son. She reached out for my help.

I explained to Ellie that she was a natural medium. Spirits were being drawn to her because she had the ability to help them. I taught her how to understand their needs and how to take control of the situation. Surprisingly, it only took a few weeks to reinforce her understanding and to give her the tools to help these souls.

Shortly, she was able to decrease the medication she was on. She was able to secure a part-time job and she didn't feel fearful all the time. Now, a few years later, she's in a healthy relationship. She's gone back to school to get her degree, and I recently received notification that she's secured a good PR job for a large firm. Most importantly, she realized that her son also has her same abilities, and due to her understanding and training, she's determined to help him get a handle on his abilities early so that his experience is not as difficult as hers was.

Not everyone goes through this hijacking of their abilities the way Ellie and Beverly have. I didn't. I was able to open more slowly. Age has nothing to do with the awakening to your abilities. They could open early in life or later in life; the process is the same. Don't fall into fear, that's the worst thing you can do. Fear is what complicates this experience. Find a way to understand what's happening to you. If you need to find a book or a person like me, to get some answers then do so. Then you can take control in the situation. Once understood, these gifts can be fulfilling.

I'm learning that Beverly is some sort of channeler. We don't know what kind of spirits she is channeling, but we need to find out. She's developed to the point where she can hear their cries. She has to find a way to see what she can do to help them.

In this session we are uncovering another factor in the individual journeys of all souls—the influence of past lives on current lives. We find that Beverly, who is dealing with this new psychic awakening, is also struggling with important issues from a previous life. In the life as the sorceress, she was psychic and had issues regarding power. We don't know many of the details.

For 71 years of Beverly's life, she has been unconsciously pushing away her power because she was being influenced by the sorceress's self-imposed feelings of punishment for misusing her power. This has caused Beverly to feel powerless in many situations throughout her life. This push and pull has happened inside her.

Let me tell you a bit more about Beverly's power issue. She is soft spoken. She has lots of views and opinions but she doesn't risk sharing them. She avoids confrontation. She is repelled by loud-voiced, big-personality people with "tin ears," people who don't listen and have already made up their mind. She is more comfortable in one-on-one situations or small groups. She is an artist who leads a very quiet life where she pursues internal intellectual interests such as printmaking, reading, family genealogy, and textile design work.

These behaviors appear to be *personality traits*, but these traits are based in beliefs and emotions left over from the sorceress's life of self-rejection and limitation. So who is the real Beverly?

As we hear in this session, it's time for Beverly to break away from this limiting behavior. In doing that, she is letting the sorceress be freed from this self-inflicted self-abuse of denouncing of her power. It's not an easy road. Beverly is currently enmeshed in living a life with little upheaval. Yet, in claiming her power over the voices who are trying to override her life, and in finding ways to help herself and the sorceress to take their power back, this is where true healing happens.

Beverly is blazing the trail for all of us. We all have issues with past lives that affect how we are living our current lives. Our goal is to find the issues holding us back, heal them, and bring balance into all of our lives. We are not on this journey alone.

All of the above is what I have concluded about the session and the wonderful training I got out of it. On a personal level, I have been increasingly worried about Beverly and all the drama and trauma these voices are causing for her. In the next chapter, I'm so worried that I pull out my Get Out of Jail Free card and call on someone who might be able to help.

Personal Growth Questions:

1. Knowing that the emotion of fear can hurt you, what do you do to distance yourself from falling into fright? How proactive are you in chasing it away?
2. Have you updated your fears lately, or are you still stuck with your old traditional ones? Is it time to clean house and throw out the trash?
3. Is automatic handwriting an end in and of itself or is it a temporary means to an end? What's the purpose?

Calling in the Big Guns

September 1, 2010, Beverly's Mindset

Well, I did it again. This time my second trip to the hospital's mental ward cost me a week. This morning I pleaded with the powers that be to hurry with my dismissal paperwork so I could get to my previously scheduled appointment with the beautician. Finally, at noon, I was released just in time to arrive directly at the beauty shop for my perm. How wonderful to see myself again in the mirror with clean, soft curls. What a boost to my morale! Going back home was a treat. After taking a warm shower to get rid of the smelly chemicals used in curling my hair and changing into clean clothes after a week in the hospital, I began to feel like myself again. Alas, not for long.

I tried to stay bright and engaged in working around the house, but I was gradually worn down. By late afternoon, my thoughts began to be disrupted by unwelcome voices. When the darkness of the autumn evening took over the sky, I turned on one light in every room to reduce my fear of the possibility of the voices suddenly being able to show up in physical form. I had never seen ghostly forms before, and worried perhaps tonight might be the night it would start.

What was I to do about my discomfort? I hated the idea of giving in to my distress as much as I hated the idea of calling Kym for help. After all, what could she do from two hundred miles away? However, I was spooked enough that I wanted to hear the voice of someone who wouldn't think I was imagining things. The phone rang. Wow! Kym called me! She said, "Are you okay? I can't get you out of my mind."

I told her about my woes. Thankfully, she didn't make light of me. She told me she would contact someone who could verify my situation. She'd call me back when she was more informed. In the endless minutes while I waited for her return call, I decided to turn on all the lights in the living room and push the recliner into the center of the room. If there was to be trouble, I didn't want to be trapped in a corner in the dark. With the television blaring, I tried to sleep as I waited for Kym's return call.

Kym's Mindset:

I was concerned for Beverly, so I phoned Elizabeth, a fellow psychic who is versed in possessions. We felt that Beverly was not dealing with a typical case, and that more clarity was needed. Next, I requested information from Jesus.

Kym (K) and Jesus (J)

K : Jesus, I would like to talk about Beverly Hafemeister's problem with voices in her head. Can you give me insight as to what is happening and why? [*My head started hurting, which is a sign to focus my attention around the head. I'm given a vision of a knitted cap with ear flaps but only the right flap hanging down over my ear.*]

J: Your understanding is not complete, like the cap with only one ear covering.

K: Okay, then help me to understand as completely as I am able to understand at this point in my growth. [*My head pain shifted to the forehead, and that's the sign of ghosts in the room. I feel ghosts are clamoring to talk to me, so they are causing me pain.*]

[*to the ghosts*] STOP! I want to talk to Jesus here. Please wait your turn!

Okay, Jesus please give me clarity.

J: Beverly has worn her aura thin in places. She has allowed this through her depression, loneliness, and leaving her body. She leaves her body seeking out her friend, Hal, to feel connection to him. Being out of her body for these trips has allowed her protection to wear thin. I'm not saying that communion with Hal is wrong, for it is not. She is not properly protecting herself, which has caused all these other souls to affect her. Many people, Beverly included, are vacating their bodies due to grief and loss, which allows spirits with the ability to move into her aura to do so.

K: Is she possessed?

J: *Possession* is a strong word where the body is invaded and controlled. On the other hand, *obsession* is where only the aura is invaded and intrusively influenced.

In Beverly's case, it's really obsession. Her thoughts are being unduly influenced. When Beverly leaves her body unattended and returns to have all these thoughts and voices in her head, these spirits are hell-bent on staying in her aura.

K: Do they have evil motivations?

J: They are making a feeble attempt at regaining a normal life without a body. You have to understand, in order for a ghost to live again, they feel they need a body, so they will seek out a host. Once in the aura, they will snatch their power by disempowering the host into feeling lonely, isolated, unwanted, dejected, and weak. At this point the host easily gives over control to anyone who will stop their emotional pain, even a voice. The ghost is given a sense of power.

Ghosts will say and do anything to keep Beverly off-balance, doubting herself, her God, and her own belief system. When Beverly is strong and spiritually connected, she is happy, full of love, and acceptance, which doesn't play well with the ghosts having the power they need to stay. They will do whatever is needed to keep her weak and powerless. They are not the devil; they are scared souls who are trying to survive somewhere. Let's say, they have dug their heels in. They find people like Beverly to influence.

K: Is Beverly crazy? I don't think she is, but does she need medication to keep these voices at bay?

J: No! Beverly is not crazy! There are so many people out there who have been diagnosed as crazy, split personality, bipolar, and all the thousands of other labels the medical professions use. You and Elizabeth [*a fellow psychic and nurse practitioner*] have discovered they are not crazy or mentally challenged. Some of them are either dealing with undue influence in their aura like Beverly, or fully possessed in the body. Some powerful and stubborn entities are living in their auras or bodies, keeping them off-kilter, which causes the misdiagnosis.

I'm glad you see that Beverly is not crazy. I'm also glad you have heard Beverly's concerns and are taking them seriously. Understanding is important for people going through this ordeal. In comparing notes with Elizabeth's experiences, you both have been learning important and valid concepts, both for your own growth and for your clients' lives.

K: Okay, so if Beverly is not crazy, yet she has attached spirits influencing her, what can we do to help both Beverly and these spirits? How can we release these spirits? How can we teach Beverly to stay free from visitors?

J: Cleanse her body out.

K: How?

J: With clear beverages, but only for one day.

K: But Beverly is just out of the hospital, will that really be good for her?

J: Yes, it will be fine. It's only for one day.

K: I lost connection …

Email Note Attached to the Recording for Beverly:

I have sent this on as it was told to me. I feel something has put a wall between me and Jesus to block me. I'm going to talk with Elizabeth this evening, and we will see what I can do to move these blocks out of the way. I knew you would be waiting for a reply, so I didn't want to delay. Let me get more information before you start the one-day cleanse. Let me get all the information before you try anything. Okay?

— Kym

Beverly's Personal Journey:

What's the hold up? Why is it taking Kym so many hours to get back to me tonight? What's she doing? Whose advice does she want? At this late hour, I can't imagine they're thrilled to answer the phone to discuss a stranger's peculiar situation. Or maybe they can't think of any solution.

Finally, the phone rang. Kym explained that she talked to a colleague and her guides, recorded the message, and prepared an email for me. To ease my fears, she called to read the message to me rather than have me wait to get to the library computer.

I was stunned by what I heard! A communication with Jesus! What? How or where do I file that in my brain? Is this another sick joke like a few months ago when "Jesus" supposedly condemned me for my blessing? Being suspicious of false voices, had I not heard these words from Kym, a trusted, recognizable voice on the phone, I would have dismissed this letter. But as I listened, his instructive words made sense and the clear liquid cleansing remedy was understandable. A yucky parallel is knowing the preparation for a colonoscopy begins with such a cleansing.

I crossed the hurdle of accepting the cause of the ailment and being okay with the gentle treatment. I next wrestled with my Doubting Thomas dilemma. Do I really believe it's the Biblical Jesus? Knowing that healing hinges on mindset, what beliefs am I holding? Without delay, the first activity of the next day was to purchase clear apple juice.

Kym's Professional Journey:

I was really getting weird vibes about Beverly. I hadn't talked with her for a while, but she kept popping into my mind over a period of days, so I called to check up on her. She wasn't doing well.

I decided I would go over Timingo's head and go to someone higher up the food chain. I settled on Jesus, who has a tendency to pop in and out of my life at random times. I figured I'd return the favor and call on him on my time schedule. Not surprisingly, he picked up!

Beverly was just out of the hospital when the voices drove her into great turmoil. I trusted it would get better, but it wasn't happening as quickly as I had hoped. I can't say Jesus's insight didn't scare me a bit. But I certainly was glad he validated my feelings that she wasn't crazy or physically possessed, something I had never believed anyway, but validation is always good.

Jesus references a nurse practitioner, Elizabeth. When we first met, she was already a trained psychic. She came to me as a student for advanced training as a medical intuitive. After the training, she was opened up to a new specialty I myself didn't have. She could look into a person's eyes and see if they were possessed.

Elizabeth is a western-trained professional, and works in a center for people with medical diagnoses of bipolar disorder, schizophrenia, dissociative identity disorder, mood disorders, and so forth. Her job is to meet and evaluate clients and fill medications for them. After her new psychic opening ability, her medical job became a moral dilemma. She could tell that some of her clients were not mentally ill, but were being heavily influenced by ghosts or spirits. She, in good conscience, could not prescribe medications to deal with an illness that was not the cause of the antisocial behavior. The dilemma she faced was therefore determining how she could assist those possessed without causing more problems for both the client and herself.

It has been a difficult road for Elizabeth. To this day, neither of us know what her ability is called. She struggles daily with the conflict between what she knows and what she is supposed to do. Elizabeth has reached out for help in her profession only to be shut down. She is going for her second master's degree and wants to write her dissertation on this topic, but was unable to find a mentor in the medical profession who would support the research. Again, shut down. We found it a great comfort to know that Jesus was aware of her plight and was able to validate her ability.

This brings up my concern over the limitations of our western medical profession's limited understanding in this area of possession and undue influence. Beverly, Ellie, and Elizabeth's clients all were stymied because of the medical profession's lack of inquisitive research in this area.

Just as Jesus gave us understanding here, in the next chapter we get very clear understanding that we have lots of help on the other side and tools available to us to maneuver in this place we call Earth.

Personal Growth Questions:

1. Think back to a time when you felt depressed and disconnected from the world around you. Could you see how vulnerable you were at that low point?
2. How do you feel about being unduly influenced by anyone or anything, let alone a ghost or entity?
3. What's your attitude towards ghosts wanting to take up residence in another person's aura? Anger, compassion, a desire for revenge? What's triggering your feelings? What's your opinion of the host? Are they weak-willed, a victim, empathetic, a sinner?

Sorting Out the Voices

October 27, 2010, Beverly's Mindset

I'm managing to keep my head above water since the frightening evening in September when Kym came to my rescue with a letter from Jesus. Since the last reading, I drove alone a thousand miles to visit my sister and travelled out of state for a high school class reunion weekend. My health regime of biofeedback, chiropractic, energy healing, and a half hour check-in with the psychiatrist all went without a flaw. A few luncheon chats with friends and stimulating weekly book discussions with our intimate church group kept me socially involved. Plus, there was a little professional sewing to be done. Yes, there were bothersome voices, but I coped pretty well. However, it's time to get a reading just to get the view, or review, of how the other side thinks I'm doing. Hopefully, they'll offer some suggestions for me to consider.

Beverly (B), Kym (K), and Hal (H)

K: Hi Bev, good to hear from you. I got your email, and you want to go over some dreams? We can do that. Do you just want to start?

B: Great. I had a dream a couple of weeks ago where I was swimming a lazy sidestroke in a lake. Water is a spiritual symbol for me. I felt seaweed attached to my shoulders that slowed my progress. Did Cherith send the dream to me?

K: He's here, and yes, the dream is twofold. Doing the sidestroke, you're not fully committed. You are only half in the water, leisurely swimming to your destination. You haven't made a commitment to *the work*. You brought the seaweed with you. It's your tangle, your indecisiveness, your worry, and concern. Flip your body down into a strong Australian crawl or breaststroke. The attached seaweed will slide off after you make a commitment.

B: Am I doing the sidestroke currently, or have I been doing it my whole lifetime?

K: Your guide is telling me you flip-flop; he's not saying that you've been noncommittal your whole life. You do the normal breaststroke, then you flip to the sidestroke.

B: A lot of subtle information is packed into one little dream! Maybe you can give me the hidden messages in another dream I had where I was the pilot of a cargo plane. Cherith was my copilot. Before departing, I walked through the plane to check the freight to see if we were ready to take off. In the tail section I was stunned to discover stowaways camping. They were not miscellaneous individual travelers, but an extended family of all ages living in the rear of the plane. I was ashamed and embarrassed for carelessly performing my job, and humiliated for bungling my task.

My interpretation of the message is that a lot more is going on than I realize as I travel through my life. I should pay attention to what's hidden under my nose. I have a copilot in my spirit guide, but I'm in charge.

K: I feel your guide is taking you in baby steps. There's a lot more connection to the stowaways than you think.

B: I can't think of anything I'm in charge of where I wouldn't notice a smattering of family members right under my nose, so I react more to the shame of needing to take baby steps at my age.

K: Why should you be ashamed? Note that you said a minute ago that the pilot in the dream felt ashamed. The dream points out to you the habitual, internalized shaming you do.

B: Truthfully I shouldn't feel ashamed, but I do. I'm a bit long in the tooth to be taking baby steps.

K: Dreams are important communication from our guides. All dreams need to be analyzed. Take note of clothing, surroundings, and demeanor of all the actors in the dream. Their clothing and speech style help to identify a time frame. Most importantly, note how you feel in the dream. Your guide exposed all of these details to you for some important reason. Look for the core, valuable message.

B: May I ask another question about dreams? I know you said I should take note of the clothing, but could this be an indication of a past life, or is that assuming too much?

K: When I started doing past life work, I had a few misconceptions. First, there was the time factor. Sometimes the past life didn't fit my notion of sequential time, so I would dismiss the information. Second, I got confused, believing an actor in this life—say my father—would be playing the same role in my past life.

For example, in a dream I was a young girl in the late 1920s. When interpreting it, I was stumped by how I could be alive in the 20s when my own mother from this life, Maureen, hadn't yet been born. She was scheduled to be born in 1936. I disregarded this past life's insight because I thought my mother in this life was playing the same role as my mother in the previous life.

Through investigation I found Maureen wasn't in the mother role in the 20s life. She was playing the role of my grandmother in that life! It's not a sequential timeline, nor are the people in this life playing the same roles in previous lives.

B: I see how that could be confusing. Here's another angle about people playing roles. Throughout my life, I've gotten unexpected feelings of familiarity when meeting a few strangers. Sometimes favorable, sometimes not. Once the bond was so strong with a fellow summer art fair exhibitor, I almost grabbed her hand and said, "Oh, you were my sister! How have you been?" I stopped myself, fearing she'd think I was nuts. I looked at her pleasant face. I looked at her beautiful textile handwork. I sensed her radiant personality and answered my own question. She had been just fine. Decades later, I'm still touched by the loving connection I felt for a supposed complete stranger.

K: Yes, sometimes our guides orchestrate sweet treats for us, like you revisiting your former sister. Other times it's not so sweet when we're given sensations to bring our attention to some unhealed past life issues. Usually the sensation shows up as a fear we need to examine.

B: I rarely examine my fears, yet inklings tell me I have a few more fears than the average person. Perhaps it is time to look.

One example of the sensation of fear without obvious reason happened in my college history class. My college history professor, by simply mentioning the name of the Italian Dominican friar Savonarola, chilled and terrified me. Fear rang a bell deep inside me, especially when I realized the friar campaigned against secular art and culture during the Renaissance. As a liberal-minded art student from the Midwest, I didn't gravitate to him. Furthermore, rigid, narrow religious views never appealed to me. Yet, why the flash of panic that accompanied hearing his name for the first time? Do you think I was an artist who was persecuted by Savonarola?

K: Well, it's one possibility. People are much more comfortable thinking they are the victim than thinking they might actually be the perpetrator.

B: Okay, but I felt chilled and frightened when I heard Savonarola's name. Wouldn't that be how a victim would feel?

K: Suppose you, Beverly, were Savonarola in that life. Your soul as Savonarola has evolved since the fifteenth century. Your reaction of shocking fright could have been a reaction to seeing your old behavior!

Back then, your guide, Cherith, just gave you a sensation to let you know there is some link between you and Savonarola. A past life reading could help you. In this type of session I describe the life to you with your behaviors highlighted without all the emotions. If and when you are ready to look at it, let me know.

B: I don't know if I'd be ready for that. My current life is bizarre enough which brings up another odd thing that happened a week or so ago. On the rare occasion I can hear my guide, he recently gave me an intense teaching on a former life. In the past life, I was a farmer involved in an accident with the conveyer belt at haying time. My son was killed and I injured my foot so badly it remained twisted. I blamed myself for my beloved son's death, never forgave myself, and sunk into a life-long depression. My wife never forgave me either. I didn't recall the teaching until this past week when I passed a redheaded man in church who had the same energy I had in a former life.

For two Sundays in a row in church, my guide arranged for me to see the redheaded man with the same feeling that I had when I was the farmer. He looked deeply depressed and had a twisted foot. I managed to reach him after the service with the goal of giving him a friendly smile to see how he would respond. I was sad to see it was hard for him to respond even for a moment of lightness. So, this was what my energy looked like in the farmer life?

K: Your guide is telling me he sent that man as validation, not for confusion. You're not psychically picking up the details of the redheaded man's life. However, there is a similar essence you, as the farmer, shared with him. It might be his depression, his lack of self-forgiveness, or his self-loathing. Thus, his look is familiar.

Essences have specific, concentrated vibrations. Many people might call this a "vibe," which we can read from across a room. You picked up the essence that was familiar in your past life as the farmer. Like an identifying marker, it's the way the human mind works. We fill in the blank spaces. Your mind filled in the blanks that the redheaded man you saw looked like you as the farmer.

B: We pick up their essence to remember our past, right?

K: Yes, your guide's smiling right now. You understand. Do you have another question?

B: Yes, I have another one. I've grown to appreciate my mother, father, and sister in this life. Have they been with me before?

K: Yes, you've been together lifetime after lifetime, always as players in each other's lives. The intense relationship you have together as a family unit keeps you coming back to help each other. Most people are like that, it's not unusual. Your guide sees it as a repertory theater with the same actors in a multitude of plays. These are your favorite thespians you put in different roles. Your mom, your sister, and your dad are repeatedly engaged in your different lives, but not every life. Likewise, you play parts in their lives too.

B: My family is making wonderful progress. They are a gift to me in this lifetime.

K: Your guide is saying to me, "See what she says. Her family is making progress which implies she's not. She's putting a mirror on the very issue she has, which is self-loathing. She thinks she's not doing as well as they are."

B: "Self-loathing?" What a harsh word! I don't see that at all! In fact, I don't believe it!

K: Beverly, that's what your guide is pointing out, and I'm sorry to say, but it's his job to help you consider things you don't want to see about yourself. However, I feel your self-loathing issues are not only from this life, but are carried over from a past life.

B: What could I have possibly done in a past life to despise myself so completely? Was I some kind of a monster? Maybe this self-loathing might explain another experience I had, which I never confessed to you. At church, during an audience response time came the loudest, deepest wail of pain I had ever heard. Where did the noise come from? In panic I looked around the congregation to see their reaction. My jaw dropped. I alone heard it.

Such a dreadful screech in my head weakened me to the point where I almost collapsed from the horrible sound! This was totally different from any sound I had heard before. The voices had never given such a wail of deep agony. Was this scream me? Was I causing myself distress? At the time, I felt somehow involved. Logically, I had no idea what I could have done to cause this intense pain. Is my soul traumatized because of me or my actions? I never knew there was so much turmoil buried inside me. Was that dreadful scream in my head a spirit attachment or my own self-loathing?

K: No, this is not a case of spirit attachment. Part of your soul cannot forgive itself, so it can't find wholeness! Those are advanced questions. People don't think they should ask their guides, "Why do I have this trait, habit, or behavior?" Past lives can help explain all of them. They might be small, minor things.

B: What do you mean?

K: This is a new topic we've never talked about before: *soul fragments*. You have to know that you, Beverly, were not the cause of your soul's pain. Timingo says our souls, including yours, are split into multiple pieces. Each fragment has a separate life. Each soul fragment makes their own choices, and has its own consequences. Some choices have consequences which cause pain. You, as a member of this soul fragment collective, can sometimes feel other fragment's pain. In this case you heard a piercing scream belonging to a soul fragment in your collective.

Have you ever had a situation where you felt depressed, yet nothing in your life could have caused that feeling? Well, the feeling of depression could be overflowing from your soul fragments.

Honey, your guide is telling me you are not yet ready to understand the depth of this teaching. Let's leave it here. We'll revisit it at a later date. Is that okay?

B: Yes, I need to process this new information. Let's talk later when I can digest more. But frankly, in all we have discussed today, I'm shocked by the criticism of self-loathing. Why would I not think I had caused the pain since the wail was only in my head, unheard by the congregation? Why wouldn't I think I was being personally addressed?

K: I don't know, but you need to trust your guides on this. Our guides are a perfect match for us. They know how to help us in the best way. They collaborated with us on structuring our lives in all aspects, all lifetimes. They give us bite-size pieces we can swallow. You need to stop knocking yourself! Don't put the shame judgment upon yourself as much as you do. See your guide's wisdom in knowing your needs and helping you when you are ready to understand.

B: That's how I need to start looking at it.

K: Cherith just identified your struggle with self-loathing, which damages your self-love. To combat this self-loathing issue, you need to find acceptance in your talents, intellect, and kindness by loving yourself. Pay attention to your self-image view, which you intellectually understand, but struggle to implement in your life. Think about it. See if he's right, then modify it. You'll thank him for it.

B: On the self-loathing diagnosis, intellectually I don't agree. Emotionally, I'm surprised and hurt the guides haven't sensed that I like myself and appreciate myself, because I do.

K: We can intellectualize things, but we can't always believe them in our hearts. You're not making the connection in your heart yet about your damaged self-image. I'm sorry to say I recognize your self-judgment essence, too.

Beverly, I also struggled intellectually with my own lack of self-love. I knew I had common sense and the ability to figure things out, but I didn't value those abilities because I didn't love myself. Could I see any real goodness in me? No, I could not. I started to pay attention to everything I said about myself in my head. I was appalled!

The turning point came when I stopped my negative self-talk of rejection and put-downs. It was hard, especially since my family dynamics reinforced snarky behavior. As I listened to what I said in my head and what came out of my mouth, I became hypersensitive. I would not allow others around me to talk negatively. In this process, I changed both myself and, as an unexpected bonus, my family dynamics also changed. Beverly, I stopped and listened, so must you. Watch everything you say and think about yourself. See what you find, then do something about it.

B: You mean all the negative voices I hear talking are mine?

K: Could very well be. First, we need to sort out what your negative self-talk is. Next, see what is being said by other entities, be it ghosts, crossed-over spirits, or your spirit guides.

Step 1: Become super conscious of every thought. Think about what you think about.

Step 2: Identify and list your habitual negative self-talk in order to identify what comes from you. Take action to stop this habitual behavior.

Step 3: Take note of any off-the-wall remarks that could not be attributed to the way you think or speak. Someone, such as a ghost, might be pushing your hot buttons.

Step 4: Are you hearing kind, loving, helpful, encouraging support over an extended period of time? These are your family and loved ones. They're crossed-over spirits.

Step 5: Are you getting insightful, problem-solving information? It's your spirit guide.

Once you separate out all the above, fine-tune your perception by seeing what might be coming from your past lives and soul fragments. At first, the voices and thoughts in your head all sound like you, but when you really listen, you will become aware that each voice has a different sound. Depending on how they speak, you'll start to identify them.

B: So you thought it was just you talking to yourself?

K: Yes, I thought it was my own voice. I never entertained the possibility that it wasn't me. I was quite surprised when I realized it was my spirit guide, Timingo, talking to me.

Hal is here. I'm feeling great compassion coming from him, because you're one of his important people.

H: You want to think it's all or nothing. "Are all of these voices spirits talking to me?" or, "Are all these voices just me talking to myself?" but it's actually a combination. Your job is to sort them out.

For a while, doing automatic handwriting, we were having a grand time, but soon things started overriding the sessions. Other entities were sliding in between the two of us. Spirits were popping in, but much of the disruption was your own negativity from your past lives. You have lifetimes of your own unfinished business sliding into the automatic handwriting, which feels like a separate entity! In essence, it is another life, but they're your lives!

K: Wow! What's new to me is realizing our past lives can slide into our current life. Maybe that's why your guide has exposed past lives to you, like the farmer. Now we can put this all together. The voices are not all outside entities, they're also your own unhealed, unfinished parts from your past lives.

This material has been pretty dense, why don't we take a break here and start again tomorrow?

B: I agree.

Beverly's Personal Journey:

The takeaway message from this reading is how our spirit guide bombards us with symbols to anchor us to everyday events. Knowing how few dreams actually register in my conscious mind, I'm impressed he uses dream symbols continually to connect me to my real Earth life. Furthermore, he wants me to observe both the happy and the troubling past.

During this session my guide spotted and responded to my fleeting emotions—not my words—about my family "making wonderful progress." He was correct. I distinctly recall a split-second flash of envy towards my family, so fast it hardly registered in my mind before I responded, yet he caught it.

How does it feel to have a spirit guide that perceptive and honor bound to make me face truths I'd rather not see? My answer, with a gulp, is "fine." His job description requires fair assessment. My job is to consider his insight and tweak my life accordingly. His verdict of self-loathing is extremely harsh to hear, but he's plopped it down on the table in front of me to examine when I can muster the courage.

Kym's Professional Journey:

I love this chapter. We see throughout some of the tools our spirit guides use to get information to us: dreams, symbols, essences such as the redheaded man, and the recognition of someone from a past life such as the woman at the art show. Each are a wonderful example of how our guides, who are a part of this invisible structure, help us along the journey to enlightenment.

In this chapter, Beverly's spirit guide brings up her life theme of self-loathing. Sometimes our guides have to tell us things we don't want to hear, as Beverly can attest!

A repetitive lesson for Beverly included in her life theme also has a common link which many, if not all, people share. It's discernment. In Beverly's case, it's pretty extreme due to her psychic ability, but many of us also hear negative thoughts in our heads that all sound like our own voices. Or, we might hear our mom's or dad's voice of judgment that we heard over time. Have you ever thought to listen to these thoughts and identify their source? Are they still valid? I have found something said to me when I was five years old was still bouncing around in my head when I was fifty-five years old! Really? Why don't we spring clean these old judgments out?

Many years ago, when I was starting to build a relationship with Timingo, he taught me one of the most important lessons of my life: "Think about what you think about." I first heard that phrase from *Conversations with God,* by Neale Donald Walsch, but the real teaching came from Timingo. He'd say it to me when I was caught up in negative thoughts about myself, which was just about everything I thought. I lived with a looping tape of personal slams against everything I said and did. Never judgmental about others, I was too busy being judgmental about myself. Timingo's consistent prompting with this statement was the pivotal shift I desperately needed to get off the hamster wheel of self-abuse.

I wasn't hearing voices like Beverly, but the tapes I was playing and listening to over and over again in my head were the voices of people in my life: my mom, my teachers, my stepdad, and old boyfriends who came in and out of my life. The discernment I had to learn was not so much what others said about me, but what I was reading between the lines of what I perceived people were saying that was the real damage. "You're not good enough," "You're so lacking you have to do twice as much as others just to break even," "You're stupid, fat, and unlovable," and so forth.

By finally listening to what I was thinking, it allowed me to hear the horrible words I said over and over again to myself. I was alarmed by what I heard and soon realized I was believing stuff that was not true. Reader, I wish to hand over that gift of self-awareness to you. I hope you will take time to "think about what you think about." See if what you're thinking is empowering you or disempowering you.

Remember Timingo's nagging. He constantly reminds us to be aware of our beliefs and motivations, and to make modifications that bring us to enlightenment.

In the next chapter, we delve into the past life of the sorceress and Bev's life theme of self-loathing. It's going to be a bumpy ride!

Personal Growth Questions:

1. Do you remember any dreams? Do you make an effort to analyze them? Have you wondered why they come to you and what their purpose is? If you haven't paid attention to your dreams, are you more inclined to rethink your decision after reading this chapter?
2. Did it give you pause to consider you might be a perpetrator rather than a victim when you have a reaction to a name such as Beverly did to Savonarola?
3. Think about what you think about.

Who's in Charge of Me?

October 28, 2010, Beverly's Mindset

All kinds of entities have the ability to express their opinions to me; none wear muzzles. I've been slow to comprehend this concept. Yesterday's session gave me well defined differences between those who might be speaking to me. If I picture myself walking down busy Main Street while an assortment of uninhibited spirits stroll past me, eager to express their random viewpoints—good, bad, or indifferent—this imagery might be beneficial to keep me grounded. I'm past the age in this life to do the bidding of everyone I see walking by. I sort through opinions and reflect on those that resonate with me. Why do I still fall into the belief that unseen speakers are all truth-tellers with divine knowledge? Why have I been willing to take all of their opinions seriously just because I can't see them? The belief is absurd, but that's exactly what I've been doing unwittingly.

Kym (K), Beverly (B), and Cherith (C)

K: Okay Beverly, do you have any questions for Cherith?

B: Yes. Last night, I thought of another question. Can past lives be what the doctors label "bipolar" or "split personality?"

C: Yes, mislabeling is common. Many people would benefit from an enlightened psychologist experienced in past life regressions to bring understanding to their clients' plights. It may be a road of investigation for others to find such a person, but not for you.

Beverly, you cling to fearful issues. If you went through a past life regression, which requires reliving the past with its intense emotions, you'd be too overwhelmed. Instead, I'm moving you forward in slower steps by giving you the story format, which summarizes the life rather than your re-experiencing it.

K: Cherith is right. In a past life *reading*, I relay the story to you; you're not experiencing it. Just your active listening brings the past life into your conscious mind then in some miraculous way parts of your soul heal at some level and the issue is released.

Putting you through a *regression* is different. I relax you first. Next *you* see the life. You experience it and make the emotional connection. Then, you describe it to me so I can ask questions that lead to greater understanding of the issues unresolved in that life. These two methods of revealing past lives are equally healing.

B: Cherith sure knows me! I do agree that I'm not ready for a regression. What does he think of the psychiatrist I'm currently assigned?

K: [*to Cherith*] Do you feel he's of benefit to Beverly?

B: His Middle Eastern surname name appealed to me. It implies to me he might come from a broader background.

C: Right, yet he's still limited. I'm not saying he harms you, but he plays into your fundamental fears since he's limited to his professional belief system.

B: Unfortunately, I'm stuck taking pills until I can convince somebody I'm not hearing voices, even though I am. I have to act like a normie to avoid drugs, which are not the solution.

K: I understand. The doctor was okay for your hospital needs. You were feeling alone and not totally in control. By being in the hospital, you felt safer, thus temporarily proactive, although you soon began to feel trapped and that you were still without answers. I don't think this is the first lifetime you've found yourself in mental distress.

B: I don't know about the past, but I've wondered if I've been in a mental ward or insane asylum in my history. My chiropractor referred me to a Reiki Master, a woman who specializes in removing attachments. I went, and she validated that I had outside attachments. What does Cherith think? Does he agree?

K: No, he doesn't agree.

B: She was pulling out …

C: She felt your different *lifetimes,* which are different from the energy of the Beverly personality, but they were incorrectly interpreted as attachments.

K: This is all news to me too!

B: So she temporarily got them to back off a little, because I have been feeling gradually better.

C: People tend to think that if they had three or four past lives of energy with unfinished issues, they have to go back, dredge them up, and look at them. It's not necessary in most cases. A Reiki practitioner, who has the ability, can remove unfinished issue energy that was created in a past life.

B: Seated in her office, she held my hand. I don't recall she did anything physically to me. I assumed she was healing me energetically in her head. Something left me; I felt a little lighter and told her so. She also felt something or someone had gone. She was thinking it was an attachment, but Cherith is saying she isn't right. He's putting more emphasis on the issues pulled forward from unhealed lives.

K: Reiki is for the physical body, but it can also work for spiritual healing done through energy. The woman must have sensed your past lives energetically even though she miscatagorized them.

Your guide's saying everyone experiences unfinished emotions from their past lives which play out in different ways. Your psychic hearing sensitivity facilitates you consciously recognizing your past life issues. Many people with this sensitivity find themselves in dire straits if they don't realize their voices can be past lives, soul fractures, or ghosts.

B: Can we talk about that?

K: Yes. The guides are reminding me—ghosts can behave in different ways. One method is to attach to the aura of a living person, a host, where they can influence the host's thoughts and actions. Or, ghosts can possess a living person from inside and can control that living person. Possession is a much rarer situation, and is more complex than we have time to go into in this meeting.

[*to Cherith*] What does this have to do with Beverly?

C: Beverly is not a possessed host. When her aura is thin, she is sometimes affected by obsessors, who are ghosts, but Beverly's situation is further complicated because of her psychic hearing sensitivity. Beverly is able to hear her own past lives, soul fractures, and other entities.

K: [*to guides*] How can we heal her when they are herself? Is there a way to heal previous lives so this energy can move through her and leave?

Your guide wants you to journal. For right now, keep an emotional distance. Log what the voices say. Next, have a conversation about this log with Hal, who keeps you in your intellectual base. Both of you look at it, discuss any fears that arise, and write down your conclusions for review.

B: Am I to analyze it?

K: Yes, you and Hal both have the gift of analyzing. When you review the journal, look at it from an intellectual perspective. See what commonality these voices and thoughts share. Here will be clues to get great clarity about your core fears. Then you can take actions.

B: While in the hospital, I prayed a few long, impassioned prayers. Interrupting voices assaulted me ceaselessly by inventing ridiculous rules and regulations on proper prayer protocol, saying, "You're doing everything wrong. Your prayer allotment time is up, and God has left the office." Exasperated, I fluctuated between a flood of tears and bitter chuckles. I felt frustrated, powerless, and abandoned. This harassment went on and on every time I attempted to speak quietly to God. To me, the privacy of prayer was sacrosanct, so I was frustrated by the severing of our communication.

Since returning home, the assault has continued. Now my prayer and meditation space is wallpapered by energies I have to keep rejecting but don't know how to remove. Instead, I fled from my agenda.

Now, Cherith informs me I've been hearing aspects of all my own leftover negative statements and attitudes from previous incarnations! If I had a clue, I missed it!

K: Right, they are from the past. You have a core fear attached to psychic abilities from five lives ago.

B: Yes, I want to talk about that past life. I understand I lost my power. What does power mean, my ability to stand up for myself?

K: Well, that's one superficial definition. Actually, our deep core internal power is the awareness of being a powerful God-creature.

With you, something drastic happened five lifetimes ago where you developed deep damage to your internal power core that greatly affected all your lives since then. You're still struggling with the aftermath.

B: Details, please.

K: I'm asking the guides to clarify what they mean by power. [*pause*] You were a very powerful female, a sorceress.

B: Is this psychic power we're talking about?

K: Yes, but the sorceress also manifested things through her hands.

B : I've read about Atlantis where the women manipulated balls of energy. Is that it?

K: Yes, but I don't know much about the Atlantis civilization. I'm having a weird sensation. I'm feeling energy shooting out of my hands, and I'm tingling all over as a demonstration of her ability to shoot creation energy out of her hands.

B: When I was extremely sick with rheumatic fever at the age of nine, I remember—in a rather delirious state—tossing balled energy between my hands. During the months of illness, several times a huge ball of energy from a distance crashed into my forehead. Maybe these were past life skills I was reliving?

K: Maybe. Pretty cool skills if you ask me! The sorceress felt that she had done something wrong and shut down all of her skills. That she was willing to consider her actions implies she had some redeeming qualities.

B: She chose to shut it down?

K: I don't think her power was taken from her. It was repelled by her. With her strong ego, she may have done something that crossed the line. I feel she pushed the power away and disengaged, just as you do now.

B : After my August mental meltdown, I felt powerless. I wanted peace and quiet. I told all voices to go away.

K: Yes. You are just repeating the same reclusive attitude the sorceress did! The sorceress felt she used her abilities inappropriately. She became fearful and self-critical of her behavior in using this extreme power. I feel she internalized anger toward herself. Pushing her abilities away was her idea, not other people's notion. Because you, Beverly, pushed away your abilities in this life, you still are not whole. Humans are powerful beings with abilities, yet many people are asleep when it comes to these gifts. You're not asleep, but you still keep pushing away your gifts!

B: Is that what I've come into this life to repair? Obviously, I'm not there yet. I hardly understand what we're talking about much less how to go about fixing it.

C: Like most people, you are unaware that you already have access to the knowledge you've been seeking.

Humans don't believe they already possess abilities to access all knowledge. The Universe prods us along in tiny steps to become consciously aware that we can retrieve this knowledge at any time. Beverly, since you have access to all knowledge, the understanding you need is to know you are powerful. By taking baby steps, you are retrieving your power a little at a time. This was all planned out.

B: Since my last stay at the hospital, I've been pushing away any contact with spirit voices and I stopped automatic writing. I guess it's time to start again.

K: Cherith said the work with Hal is one step back to your power.

B: I blew it with Hal because I blew the automatic handwriting opportunity!

K: You didn't blow anything. Look at your terminology Beverly!

B: But Hal and I were progressing to the stage where I could hear his words before I wrote them! I think we were on the verge of not needing the writing.

K: Well, it was not lost, it was put off a little bit longer. By thinking you blew it, you just allowed fear to overtake you again!

B: You're right!

K: Fear overtakes you. Getting back your power is watching how you speak, how you feel about yourself, how you judge yourself. Change these to become more empowered.

B: So I need to do my focused Australian crawl.

K: Yes, you're still building your connection with Hal and your guide, who are constants in your life. Keep building those relationships.

When something feels like it's coming into your thoughts, look at it from an intellectual point of view. Remove yourself emotionally and ask, "Who's saying this to me? Why would this criticism come through?" Talk to your guide about it and ask him, "What do I do now? Where did this come from? Is this a past life? What can I learn from it? Now can we release it?" You're including your guide in the process, so you're healing.

B: How does my guide communicate with me?

K: Contact comes in many ways. As you already know, he comes through your dreams. Signs, synchronicity, knowings, promptings, and delays are indications. Don't worry, he'll get through to you. Don't have expectations, but mentally prepare yourself to be open and analytical, *not emotional,* about what you experience. Use the tool of automatic handwriting, which is one of your strong suits.

B: It was coming quite easily. You're sure it would be good to correspond again?

K: Yes, they have already said so. Use automatic handwriting with Hal, who's a big part of this journey. Your intellect needs the transcript for later reference. If and when another writer's style comes through, you'll learn to differentiate with practice.

B: Hal and I feel right. When he notices I'm switching over to someone else, can he intercept? In our June reading, Hal said he couldn't override the false messages he saw me writing. Maybe he's learned new skills by now.

K: I don't know if he's learned some new tricks. Talk to Hal about it. Say, "I want to do some automatic handwriting today. If something comes through differently than what you sent, can you help me become aware of it? Give it to me in my head or make me realize a different feeling. It doesn't matter how, I just need to differentiate between you and them." Look at this in an intellectual way, not an emotional way. Don't get upset.

B: Yes, I'd feel good about that.

K: Your guide and Hal are both nodding because you're taking power back. Taking power comes in different forms. For example, if you need help or direction, when you're asking for something in a direct and confident way, you're being empowered. Stating your intention is taking power. It's not timid, like saying, "I hope this works."

B: I took assertiveness training, so I see the difference and recognize my pattern.

K: It's all attached to your powerful sorceress life. Facing this power challenge is why you came back a timid personality.

B: It sounds like I was skilled in the sorceress work. However, I'm hearing the word "perversion," as if accused of violating some religious tenet. Do you think she did something to offend the established religion?

K: Could be. She was extremely powerful and accomplished at what she did. With power, things can go awry.

B: Will knowledge help in the healing process?

K: Yes, tell your guides, "Give me information as to why I've built so much fear around the sorceress life." Ask them, "Why have I made her hang ups into such a big ordeal that I need to work on her for so many lifetimes?"

The guides are not necessarily going to drop everything on you in one big clump. They'll take you back in small steps. Our guides work with us where we are. You're so intellectual, they'll work that way. Look at each situation from a thinking point of view. Be aware of subtle things happening. Question your guide rather than fall into your fear mode.

B: In my meltdown I ran away from any internal conversations. I felt the voices were ganging up on me.

K: They weren't ganging up on you, they wanted you to become aware of their existence. When you heard voices making negative remarks, you interpreted it as directed at you. It was not! You were overhearing the internal, negative chatter of these other lives talking to themselves in their own heads. These voices all have a pattern of negative self-talk. Your guide says you're doing the same thing when you say, "I blew it. I'm dumb. I'm embarrassed to have to take baby steps." If you stop your own negative self-talk, you're helping your other lives heal the same thing in their lives. Please understand you have been given this gift of past life awareness and you can help heal them.

Bev, I'm going to drop a complex idea on you. I'm sure you have heard it before, but like me, might not have processed it. The Universe is not ruled by time, we earthlings are. We relate everything to time, believing there is past, present, and future. It's our limitation, this time belief. Many lives we perceive as past lives are really happening at the same time as this one. Our soul fragmented in order to experience many things at the same time. We are one of those living fragments, but we also have other parts of our soul fragments alive. We do live multiple lives at one time, but please, Beverly, don't get lost in all this complexity.

To help you keep this straight, think of yourself as one of the babies of quintuplets separated at birth and all have been scattered across the world. Each quint is unaware of the other siblings. These quintuplets have similar behaviors. In this case, all express negative self-talk. Now you, Beverly, have come into awareness of your quint siblings who carry this gloomy self-talk habit. You decide to stop this behavior in your own life and, by osmosis, help your quint siblings to change their same pattern of behavior.

Beverly, draw a circle on a piece of paper to represent your soul. From the soul draw out five lines. At the end of each line make a circle and put a name: Mark, Sally, Beverly, Bill, Nancy. These represent all your soul fragments. The soul is having five different life experiences all at the same time.

A Soul With Soul Fragments

Sally gets in a horrific car accident. Her own child is killed. The impact of Sally's grief, depression, fear, guilt, and loss is felt in different ways in the lives of all the quints. All feel a reaction to the tragedy. However, none of them know where the feelings originated. As a result:

Mark becomes very depressed, yet, doesn't know why. He amps up his self-judgment behavior and acts out aggressively to those around him.

Nancy, who is a mother herself, suddenly feels a great fear around losing a child. She starts acting like a helicopter parent, which is a completely different parenting style than before. Nancy's behavior is intensified as a result of feeling her sibling's loss.

Bill, the quiet loner, is feeling isolated in ways he never felt before as a reaction to Sally's sense of loss. He now has an overwhelming need to connect with others.

Now you, Beverly, felt grief by learning your friend Hal died. Your own grief, plus the grief transferred from Sally, made this intense emotion out of proportion to the situation.

Thus, each soul fragment responds to the other soul fragments' experiences. However, as much as you can feel their pain, you can also gain from their growth. Therefore, working on your self-talk can affect how your quints modify their self-talk.

Let me show you how this all plays out with the voices in your head. When you are automatic handwriting with Hal and your funnel is open, all of a sudden, Mark's feelings come through full of accusatory, angry, ugly words which are directed at himself. You are just overhearing them.

To help Mark, do not take on his feelings. Do not personalize or convert his words to mean you. Instead, send him healing energy of self-forgiveness through comforting words such as, "we all make mistakes," "don't beat yourself up for being human," etc.

Also, remember to act out that same self-forgiveness towards yourself! That way you and all your past lives are relieved of some of your baggage. If Beverly heals, every sibling is also healed of that specific topic in their lives. It's powerful! Now add in all the other lives of that main soul, all the lives currently happening, all the lives already finished. The impact of each of these lives is being played out in bits and pieces by the five quints. The picture is more complex than we can imagine!

B: A long journey with huge implications.

K: An amazing journey! On the human level, it's hard to understand that all these things can happen at the same time. Time is the issue. We think we only do one thing at a time. We don't.

B: So we need to keep rethinking multiple experiences at the same time.

K: Yes. Didn't our guides say we are God? As God, we can split into a multitude of experiences. Some of these lives happen at the same time. It's how this game is played.

Plus, we're still working with our past lives, which give us answers to our issues in this life. In my work with past lives through regression, I find we repeat the same subject matter in many of our lives. What seems to connect the lives is the *subject matter*, not the individual details.

B: We also need to think of all the good experiences in these lives, not just the problem areas. Are these happy branches connections too?

K: Absolutely! Yet, when life is good and easy, people aren't often spurred on to grow. We learn more when we have trouble.

B: How everything fits together is amazing.

K: I'm fascinated by the complexity if we just take the time to figure it out.

I want to thank you, Beverly. By calling me for a reading, you've given me an opportunity to learn more about this topic for my own growth. I feel you were supposed to be here to help me bring forth this new information and these concepts.

B: You're welcome. These readings take me places I never thought were possible! I'll need time to process all you've shared, so, can we shift gears? [*pause*] Ask Cherith if he likes the class I go to on Thursdays.

K: He likes anything that doesn't have you fall into fear. I feel this class is positive.

I see a vision of a whirling red ball labeled FEAR; I feel this is connected to your sorceress life. Unfortunately, the ball has gotten bigger and bigger because you've added to it over lifetimes. It's bouncing directly toward you. You need to keep it away!

B: Maybe as the sorceress I was doing a lot of spectacular, powerful, and maybe frightening stuff, but something went amiss, so am I trying to undo the damage I/she, did back then?

K: With some past lives, simply by having remembrances come to our consciousness, they heal; there's nothing you have to do. With others, depending on the significance of the past life, sometimes you need to look back at that life.

My student, Mary, was devastated when she regressed into her past life as a Roman soldier, who was ordered to kill old people and children. He did. With Roman (as we named him) and Mary working together, she helped heal him and healed herself in this lifetime. They were extremes—Roman's brutality and Mary's super sensitivity to violence.

Different belief systems, different times. Mary was very upset at finding she/he perpetrated this behavior. She was judging her life as Roman from today's cultural standards, not from his environment. We can't do that. Mary had to find compassion for Roman based on how he made choices based on his life in those times. His superiors made it clear, "Kill these people or we'll kill you!" Imagine living under those norms!

B: Cultural norms affect how we view past lives.

K: Likewise with your sorceress. What cultural belief system was normal during her lifetime? Whatever it was, it strongly impacts your life negatively and is important to address. In your case, the extremes are Beverly's powerlessness and the sorceress's power. Her behavior of "I did something wrong, I'm running from it," is not healthy. Beverly, help her by embracing your power in a balanced way. Take action in this life. You have the power now. Keep the ball of fear away. Get back to the true you. We're all here on Earth to find out who we really are.

Okay, on that note, let's call it a day.

Beverly's Personal Journey:

The comfortable, little world of Beverly just got super-sized beyond my comprehension. Now I see myself as one wandering thread woven into the fabric of many other people's lives, as they are in mine. An invisible structure has us all connected to the very core. Now I must ask myself, "Why do I feel melancholy today?" Is it because it's cold and rainy and I must stay indoors? Or, maybe the feeling didn't originate with me. Perhaps one of my "quints," my soul fragments, is unwell. I find myself expressing mothering thoughts toward my unmet segments wherever they are, whatever they're facing. Now I see how we are locked together in this life to succeed independently yet together. If I have a grouchy day for a silly reason, I catch myself, apologize to my "quints" for dragging them down, give a little pep talk to all of us, and get on with my day. Suddenly, I can't crawl in a cave, lick my wounds, and sulk. This is a team sport. I have responsibilities to myself and them. If that doesn't put a new spin on life, I don't know what does.

Kym's Professional Journey:

This chapter has a plethora of information and insights to different parts of the soul's journey. We're going to look in more detail at the life theme of *self-loathing*.

As we talked in the early chapter about the outline, the life theme is the "mission" for entering into this life. The outline you design includes situations and people who will help you to experience this life theme. Each choice is made with one question: "What situations can I design to allow me to encounter my self-loathing?" You're stacking the deck *in favor* of you facing your life theme: self-loathing. Self-loathing is the filter, the colored glasses, you look through in all experiences and interactions.

First, let's clearly define self-loathing. Self-loathing is ongoing, extremely negative, judgmental internal thoughts about oneself.

But one caveat needs to be addressed here. Self-loathing or any life theme is not full throttle all the time in every area of your life. Just like the feeling of confidence, you might be very confident in your career, but you are not confident in relationships. There are varying degrees of how self-loathing plays out, but it's always there in some percentage.

For an example, let's look at how a self-loathing life theme can play out in a soul's journey:

Think about a female child, let's call her Trisha, with this theme. As a young tot Trisha displays perfectionist behavior.

She has to do things over and over again until she gets it right. If she can't do something, she is a very frustrated tot!

In addition, Trisha might *appear* highly competitive, but it is an internal competition with herself and not directed toward others. Trisha's focus in the early years are on *how she sees herself.*

As Trisha moves into her teens, she starts to *see herself through the eyes of others* and things get really difficult.

Any child moving into the teen phase deals with many changes, from hormonal to self-centered, all-about-me thinking. This phase allows ample opportunity for her to be judged by others, but for self-loathing teens, it's ten times more internal judgment. Teens are judged on how they look, the school they attend, the grades they get, the clothes they wear, the company they keep, etc. The teen phase is a petri dish of heightened experiences to conflict the self-loathing child.

Self-loathing teens are constantly amplifying their self-judgment. If her family/friends make a simple implied judgment of any sort, the self-loathing teen can lash out and/or recoil into themselves. Many self-loathing teens start cutting themselves, or restricting themselves through eating disorders. They are trying to stop or control the judgmental thoughts pulsing through their heads. Being a teen can be very hard, but for a child with this specific life theme, it's brutal!

Reader, ask yourself, "What could happen to a teen girl that would cause her to loathe herself?"

Thousands of things. How many teens are self-absorbed and feeling the world revolves around them? The teen years are a great time to get lots of experience with this or any life theme, but as one ages into their twenties, what then?

There are many ways to set up situations to continue this self-loathing life theme throughout their twenties with relationships —either romantic, or family and friends.

By their thirties, there is marriage (or divorce from a twenties marriage). Add in children. There are tons of situations that a self-loathing woman can find to beat herself up. "Am I a good wife, mother, sister, daughter, friend?"

By their forties, they have accumulated an enormous education in experiences and reactions to this life theme of self-loathing.

Around this time, they look back at the road they have walked and evaluate the way they have dealt with this life theme. They see the crashes and burns, the broken relationships, the mess that transpired due to their *reaction* to all these perfectly arranged situations. With a self-loathing life theme, they beat themselves up all the more for the mess life has become in different areas.

There is hope! The life theme needs to be experienced, but it also needs to be worked through. The second part of a life theme is: "How to experience this life theme and still have a great life?" It's all in how they *deal* with all the situations as they arise that is the important part.

To stay with the self-loathing theme, let's make up a drama. A person—let's make it a man for a change—has a great love unexpectedly come into his life. He was gaga in love with a woman, and because of his "love blindness" he didn't see some of the sketchy behavior that was going on with her. She ended up leaving him, no note or explanation, just poof gone.

True to form, this self-loathing life theme man, goes into a whirlwind of self-incrimination and a rampage of beating himself up. Self-loathing at its finest! "Why didn't I see this coming, I should have known! Of course she would be doing that stuff, because I was never enough for her! I always knew it was too good to be true! I could never have kept the attention of such a (fill in the blank) woman, she was so out of my league. Why was I kidding myself?" His tirade is very little about what she did, it was all about him! This is what the self-abuse wheel looks like. Do you recognize yourself?

Now you come into awareness about your life theme of self-loathing like Beverly did, so now what do you do?

After you "get" that you are clearly in this life theme, you need to understand that all situations are set up to help you experience this theme. Not all are "full on," they might be small touches of this theme, or maybe they are covertly hidden in the situation. Note your *reaction* to the situation.

For instance, someone might say an innocent comment to you about something. If it triggers you, you will not know that you were triggered until you listen in on your thoughts about the comment. Then watch what you want to do in retaliation—to yourself.

Only in this identification of your *reaction* can you come up with a plan on how to deal with these triggers in the future. The goal is to learn how to make the consequences to yourself less extreme in your life. Hence, you will have a better life because you are not allowing the triggers to send you on a self-loathing rampage.

In the next chapter, we have a bit of a changeup. I had a personal meeting with a famous dead author. It was another big step into a new understanding on how our belief system can cause discontent in our soul journey.

Personal Growth Questions:

1. If you want to know about your past lives, which method would you choose? (a) story narrative from a reading, or (b) regression where you see and relive that past? Why?
2. What kind of a patient are you? Do you choose to put yourself in the hands of your doctors and follow their instructions or do you choose to investigate alternatives? Is your medical community open to supporting you in investigating other options?
3. When the voices explained that Bev was "overhearing" past life personal negative head chatter and misinterpreting it as being said to her, how did this hit you?

Wanna Be a Ghostwriter —For a Ghost?

May 13, 2012, Kym's Professional Journey

In this chapter, we include a session that did not involve Beverly, but it was an interesting teaching that reflects on another aspect of the invisible structure, as you'll see.

In early May of 2012, while in meditation with Timingo, I was introduced to a classy man with a big personality wearing a tweed jacket. The man informed me he had been watching me for the last six months, trying to decide if he wanted to work with me. He finally decided I was the one he wanted. At the time, I had many experiences with ghosts, but not a working relationship with one.

I asked him why was he a ghost? He said, "Because I'm working on a karmic debt I feel can only be dealt with on the ghost level." At the time, I didn't realize we had the ability to make concrete choices for our soul evolution by becoming a ghost and clearing up our "debts," as he called them.

At the time, my writing life consisted of penning a few blogs and finishing up a first draft manuscript of a memoir on my relationship with my spirit guide, which I was writing to share only with my students. Even with this first attempt at writing, I never thought of myself as a writer. But surprisingly, I recently felt compelled to dabble at writing a few short fiction stories, which had never interested me before. Later, my new ghost friend took credit for being the one inspiring me to write fiction.

Aside from the karmic debt issue, this man with the strong ego also wanted to bring forth public awareness that he was still very much alive and creating. His scenario was to prove his point by writing through me and attributing the work to himself. He announced he was not alone in this quest; other dead authors wanted to do the same things. "Why me?" I asked.

He responded, "Being without a writing educational background, combined with your ability in the psychic field, makes you a perfect candidate to channel my work. For you, career-wise, it's not a big leap. You're already publicly known as a medium who speaks to dead people. Why not prove it by channeling fresh writing material from well-documented dead authors, starting with me? Each dead writer, who is interested in writing through you, has a unique prose that could not possibly be written *by* you, hence proof." His conviction was clear, but I wasn't so easily convinced. The idea and the consequences of following through with such a plan didn't thrill me, but I was open to seeing where this went.

I'm slightly ashamed to admit that I have not read many books outside of the self-help genre. He wrote in fiction. His fame as an author had reached me, but I had never read his work. In fact, I didn't even know his first name.

First, he wanted to teach me about the structure and habits of a focused writer, but I soon found out that, more often than not, I was instructing him about my medium work. Quickly thereafter, we became co-experiencers in the metaphysical area in which he was previously unfamiliar.

His name is Hemingway, Ernest Hemingway. You can read more about our relationship in a forthcoming book that highlights my experiences with a myriad of ghosts, including Hemmy, as I call him. But for now, here is where Hemmy and I found out about *belief clusters*.

Kym (K), Timingo (T), and Hemmy (EH)

K: Hemmy, are you around?

EH: I'm here.

K: Good. So, are we going to collaborate on something soon? I'm itching to get started! Or do I have to wait until you call on me with an inspiration?

EH: Well, you have been busy, and I see there are some spirits around you.

K: Yes, Mary, my friend and fellow psychic, phoned me today in a panic because she was accosted by some cemetery ghosts while visiting her mom's grave. They wouldn't let her leave until she helped them. I tried to talk her through a crossing, but she was too emotional and overwhelmed. Then the ghosts all showed up at my house! My house was full of uninvited visitors. I crossed over some, but I felt some motion in the back of my head and down my back, which told me not everyone had crossed. Hemmy, can you help me deal with them or get them to leave?

EH: It's funny. I don't see them, just feel them. It's more a sensing.

K: What? I wonder why that's happening?

EH: They don't seem as solid as other ghosts I've seen. They seem more like a wisp of energy.

K: Could they be fragments rather than full ghosts? Could they be residue of the ones I already crossed over? I don't know. It's all new information to me. My usual ghosts always seem to look like you, in a solid form. Let me call in Timingo and ask him. Timingo, are you here?

T: Yes, Fine One, I am. I find it interesting to listen to the talk between you and Mr. Hemingway.

K: Yes, but as you can see, we don't seem to have the answers to what we're wondering.

T: The answers are right there. I wish both of you would reach a bit further.

K: Hemmy, do you know what he means?

EH: We need to look under the surface of the question. Give me a moment and I'll dig.

K: [*I'm slowly fading towards unconsciousness.*] I see a vision of Hemmy literally pulling up a layer of sod. Oh, he's being funny with the digging deep metaphor!

I'm sensing a wispy energy as another level of ghost consciousness. It's not a full bodied soul, but a fragment of a soul stuck on a certain belief. It feels like this soul fragment is being held back by a little issue.

Hemmy, do you have insight about how to help these little soul fragment bits?

EH: I see little orbs are attached, one on top of the other, to something like a core issue. I will try to see if I can pull one off the other.

K: I see a vision of a solid red ball with semi-transparent orbs of varying colors just stuck to the next one. Do you think the center red core is the belief?

EH: Yes, that's what I surmise.

K: Well, what do we do? You don't seem to be able to get them apart. [*I see him trying.*]

EH: No, it's like they're cemented to each other.

K: Okay, maybe we should try to cross the whole thing over as one big chunk?

EH: How do you intend on doing that?

K: I don't know. First, I think I should go to the center red core belief itself and see if I can talk with it. Maybe I can sense what its story is.

[*Headache in left front forehead; I'm getting tired and feeling heavy. I have no memory of the rest of this exchange, but the recorder was still recording the conversation. I think the heavy feeling was me being taken over by a Higher Power.*]

K: Hemmy, are you still with me?

EH: Yes, just holding this thing. [*I see him with an odd look on his face, holding the cluster as it moves around in his hands.*]

A Belief Cluster

K: Okay, let me look closer. Oh, "Anger at Self" is written on the center of this red ball of belief. So, these orbs are mad at themselves?

Oh, my stomach is starting to feel weird. Something in my stomach feels coarse, rough, and dense like sand compacted with water. I guess the center red core is showing me how it feels from people who have this self-hate. Anger at Self rubs against the person to keep them agitated, irritated, and hostile, all directed inwardly. As a result, the physical sensation is a constant low grade nausea. We damage ourselves with this self-hate belief.

Okay, I dislike this feeling, so how can I help these souls with this belief? [*pause*] I hear these small soul fragments yelling, "It is real! It hurts! I'm sick!"

[*to the fragments*] You have to understand the cause of your anger is you, even if it appears to be anger at others! Can you, little orbs, understand that? [*I want to go lie down. I feel horrible.*] Okay, orbs, do you get it?

In unison I hear "Yes." [*Hemmy is still holding this thing that looks like a science class atoms and molecules mock-up.*]

[*to the fragments*] Your belief of self-anger energy is holding your soul back from fully being in the light. Even if you still hold this belief, you can still merge with the rest of the soul.

[*to Hemmy*] Let me see if I can explain how this whole cluster works. The center red ball is like a magnet labeled "Anger at Self." All the little orbs, which are soul fragments with anger issues in them, are like iron pellets that are powerfully snapped up to the big red magnet. They become tightly bound together and can't be pulled apart, as you so well know. Therefore, I think, we might need to cross the whole contraption together and let the other side deal with it.

EH: Let's see if it works.

K: [*to the cluster*] As a group, allow yourself to release, like a bouquet of balloons, and you can cross over the Anger at Self issue with you. But, you will have to deal with the anger in a karmic way on the other side. You'll have more help to figure it out over there. Can you do it?

[*to Hemmy*] I hear mumbling, I feel they're coming to an agreement. Do you feel them getting lighter in your hands?

EH: Yes.

K: [*At first, I see the entire red ball with colorful orbs start to lift slowly. The energy shifts around them and feels better as they decide to leave. The pace quickens. I see Hemmy releasing his hands from the unit. It floats upwards as if the orbs are full of helium. Hemmy and I just watch it go. It disappears.*]

[*to Hemmy*] I want to go lie down.

[*I fell asleep for a bit and woke up feeling much better. I've felt so weird ever since those cemetery ghosts showed up. This is the first time I was talking with someone on the phone and their ghosts transferred over to me.*

I'm not sure I like this new ability! It really messed up my day. But I did learn a really interesting thing about another aspect of existence.]

K: Hemmy, are you around? Can we talk about this shared experience?

EH: I have been thinking a lot about it. New levels of understanding are opening up for us both. I see you are struggling with our connection. Please, do not put pressure on yourself.

K: I don't feel your pain in my right elbow, which is my signal you're with me. I would like that pain again, just so I know you are really here.

EH: I hope we can move on from that signal and just know I am here.

K: Well, I still don't feel it. I do need it, at least for a while more. Can you please do it? If not, I'll stop this talk.

EH: Feisty!

K: Ouch! You are a character! You gave me a pain in my ankle on my funny bone! Cute! I see you can't just do as I ask, so you seem a bit feisty too!

Okay, so you're here and I'd like your input as to what happened between us earlier today. As I was reading our original transcription, I didn't remember most of this exchange. I was surprised by that. Why do you think that is? As time goes by, I'm starting to remember it in bits and pieces, but only the visuals.

EH: I'm not sure I recall it all either.

K: Okay, another trip to Timingo. Hey, Timingo, you around?

T: Always, Fine One.

K: Okay, what's going on? Why don't we recall all of it?

T: You, Kym, were involved on one level, but you were also being a channel for us on this side to help those souls, or "soul fragments," as you so wisely have called them.

T: First, you opened a door to a new level of experience by having the cemetery ghosts come to you through the phone call with Mary. You were an open source for them. Their anger—or really fear—drew them to the brighter light, which was you over Mary. Some stayed with her, but most moved to you. An example would be if she was a captain and then you, the general, walked in the room. Those that wanted the higher rank moved to you. It was just a shift of attention for these souls at the cemetery.

Because you were unaware of the higher level of energy you were putting out, you were jumped in essence. You were under the pile of the ghosts' energy. [*I see a visual of a football game pile up with me at the bottom.*] A higher level of soul crossers came to your rescue, which is why you didn't recall it all. They were "running the show" for you. They directed the action for the release.

It was a good lesson for you and Mr. Hemingway. You two are more connected on this journey than you both realize at this junction. You think it is for your own agendas. You are unaware we have our agenda, too. When you walk into situations like this, we see an opportunity to teach you and Mr. Hemingway, plus get some of our work done as well. Releasing soul fragments is an aspect of our job. Are you offended by my actions?

K: No, I'm not. Are you mad, Hemmy?

EH: No! It's an adventure! I'm enthralled with all the unknown elements of our world.

K: Oh, you feel like a little boy in a candy store!

EH: Yes! Bring it on! That was an awareness I never knew was possible.

K: Yes, I get it. I'm going to have to process this new information. Okay Timingo, what else do we need to know about this new ability of mine? How do I control it better? I hate any kind of jumpers: ghosts, spirits, and guides from your side, too! They are all jumpers to me!

T: I am watching over you, Kym. I do have your best interests at heart.

K: Yeah, but I got really ganged up on here. I got slammed when the cemetery ghosts came to me. I had to spend a bit of time talking and crossing, then I guess the soul fragments showed up. I thought I was crossing the cemetery ghosts, but then I seemed to fade out. At least that's what I'm vaguely remembering now. When I was fading, I could really have used you to jump in and tell me it's okay to go with the flow.

T: Were you concerned?

K: No, but I wasn't aware some other spirits were working through me.

T: I found you to be in no real danger, but I will try and yell louder if and when something like this presents itself again.

K: Okay, well anything else you guys want to say? I really need to get on with my day.

[*I see Timingo look over to Hemmy who shakes his head. Timingo looks back at me.*]

T: No, I think we covered it, Fine One. Any more questions on your part?

K: No, I'm getting really tired with your two energies, I think I need to lie down. Bye.

After the session, I wanted to share it with Beverly. I thought it might be interesting to her.

Email Reply from Beverly on the Sharing of this Experience:

Hi Kym,

Are you pulling my leg? You got an offer from THE Hemingway to act as his shill? You'll note I resist making any jokes about ghostwriting with him or any other author bubbling with ideas with no platform for expression. I see the temptation of the proposed collaboration, but your hesitation is wise.

I loved hearing about your adventure with Hemmy. As I understand it, the two of you discovered, metaphorically, belief clusters composed of a magnetic red ball which attracts people with a specific, undesirable, limiting belief system. They attract others with the identical destructive tendency and click together to form big belief clusters, right? Tough to break loose from a magnetic core! This strong bond sounds like another invisible natural force.

Honestly, I learned about several things, including your comfort level with Timingo. You sure don't hesitate to argue with him. When you felt you were being dumped on by overeager ghosts who located you through Mary's telephone call, you put your guide in the hot seat to get an explanation for what you thought was his lack of protective action on your behalf. Feisty indeed! Only a loving relationship could sustain that candor!

My view on the matter is our spirit guides are sometimes slow to answer our questions because, if they jumped in too quickly, they'd squash our growth opportunities. This purpose for slowing down the process is a good one, and frankly, I'm flattered to think my guides are confident enough in me to believe, "Hey, Beverly, you can figure this out." Secretly, sometimes I'm irritated because I'm impatient and want to know now!

Well Kym, you sure are one gutsy broad. Keep me posted on your happenings.

Bev

Kym's Professional Journey:

When I suggested to Beverly that we include this session with Hemmy, she was a bit cold to the idea. She didn't want to change the system we had set up with the other sessions, but I insisted we see if it would help our readers. As we worked on the book and reviewed the chapters, it became clear to us that Hemmy's session was needed to connect some of the dots with the ghost Tim. [*In chapter four*]

When lost and frightened, Tim found Beverly doing automatic handwriting with Hal. Tim and all the other "orbs" magnetically attached to Tim's belief system were willingly dragged along into Beverly's weakened aura. Hence, they were added to her voices. We didn't realize it at the time, but Tim was demonstrating to us the information we learned in this later session with Hemmy.

On a personal note I have to say I have never channeled someone famous before [*Jesus doesn't count, LOL*], nor have I ever sought to do such a thing. As in all things with this psychic ability, I don't have control over the players who seek me out!

The work Hemmy and I did was informative on many levels. Even though I was having the physical sensations of a headache to identify that a ghost was around me, it turned out it was a fragment of a ghost not the entire ghost. I didn't know that small portions were held back by their limiting beliefs. Is this issue just for a ghost, or does this apply to all souls?

These belief clusters as we are calling them have caused me a lot of concern. I know many people who have strong and limiting beliefs. I'm sure I have a few too. So how do we make sure we release these beliefs so we can cross over fully?

As much as I loved to be introduced to Hemmy, the meeting left me with more questions than I started with. He chose to be a ghost because he feels he could work on some karmic debt on that level. What kind of karma is that? Can we choose to become a ghost or not?

Karma is not an idea I know much about. Maybe because some like to use it as some sort of whipping stick for people. I hated the idea of someone keeping a list of my behaviors and then hitting me over the head with a big bag of stuff I had to pay for. Just because I don't understand or buy into the karma issue, apparently it's still something that happens for our souls. So, is karma another tool to add to the invisible structure?

At this point, I'm now understanding being a ghost has some benefits to the soul's growth, but how? [*readers, later in the series, these questions will be addressed*]

In the next chapter, we finally meet Beverly's mom, Eleanor. She helps us to understand another level of a souls evolution, where she is helping others while also healing herself.

Personal Growth Questions:

1. What do you think about not only Hemmy, but other dead authors, wanting to write through a living person?
2. If you were Kym, would you have said yes to Hemmy's proposal? Why or why not?
3. What are your thoughts regarding the explanation from Timingo about Kym being in a pileup of ghosts and her being rescued by higher soul crossers?

Mother, Please Don't Leave Me!

January 15, 2013, Beverly's Mindset

Over the period from Oct 2010 through Jan 2013, I found I was losing the fight more days than not. I was hanging onto the good days like a person on a life preserver. Over the last year and a half of hearing voices, I had ups and downs with a special kind of nagging. Someone's voice was always in my ear criticizing me, correcting me, and trying to direct me to do whatever they wanted me to do or say. Weeks would go by while I sat. I wasn't productive or even living my life. I had to get a handle on this. I remembered while working with Kym, the guides, and my family that I would have hope. With them, I was learning about my special situation and trying different things. I needed to reach out again.

After scheduling this appointment with Kym, I wondered why I had had no particular contact with her since our last reading in 2010. Curious, I reviewed my calendar notations in amazement. Two months after our last reading, I had my third and hardest hospital stay. It took place right after the church's New Year's Eve service, which included a Burning Bowl ceremony to welcome in 2011. The tradition is a symbolic burning away of a specific personal event encountered in the past year that requires forgiveness. High on my list that year was my desire to encourage peaceful healing for the ghost,

Tim, and the removal of similar pesky spirits who continued to visit me.

At midnight, my friend Gloria, her daughter, and I joined the huge auditorium packed with congregants writing their emotionally ladened experiences ready to be discharged in a flash by using a magic paper. The collective energy was intense. One by one we filed up to the bowl to release our old experiences by holding the magic paper over the candle in the bowl, watching as our concerns flashed into brightness and immediately vanished into nothing before our eyes. It was a symbolic ritual I liked. Learning from the old, releasing the past, and moving into the new year with a clean slate and no old baggage. Perfect.

The evening had been nice, but intense. I was tuckered out the next morning because I'd never learned the art of sleeping in. Fatigue, my first warning that my aura is thin, is a slippery slope that leads to losing my balance with the voices. Just wishing to get rid of my voices wasn't enough for they're still here. I guess I wasn't clear to send my major nemesis flashing away into the air. Too much of my life's task of dealing with the voices hadn't yet been examined deeply enough, so I couldn't consider it old baggage to release yet.

Within four days of the new year I deteriorated further. Sitting in my house minding my own business, a vision hit with full sight and sound. Loud, powerful, and intimidating. I was startled as I heard with my ears the "VROOM! VROOM!" and saw with my eyes a vision of a motorcycle gang coming directly at me out of nowhere. They were coming to get me! Sight and sound, it was really happening. All logic went out the window. Panic overtook me, leaving me confused and scared. Who do I call for help? Terrified, I wondered if I should call 911 or call an ambulance directly.

Then I felt a shift from panic to logic. I got out the yellow pages and seemed to comparison shop the ambulance companies. I felt the vision start to fade some. I phoned the ambulance. As soon as it arrived, I entered the vehicle only to have the vision disappear completely. Duped again!

Buyer's remorse set in immediately. Why didn't I just tough it out and not call for help? Why did I debate with myself how to get an ambulance and never reason if it was necessary? A full load of my own angry words were dumped on me. Now I was stuck. No turning back.

All the way to the hospital I was bombarded with my own angry thoughts, which were joined by voices in my head chattering about how incompetent the ambulance crew was. "Tell them!" they yelled. "They don't know how to draw blood or take your pulse. Tell them!" Any and all words to keep me in a state of high anxiety bubbled forth. Fortunately, I had enough sense and control to keep my mouth shut, but hospital trip number three had begun for me.

The rest of the interim years when Kym and I had no contact contained up and down experiences of troubling days for me. Nevertheless, some pleasant, busy work days let me recreate some challenging draperies for three historic house museums in the Midwest. As for today, I don't know what to expect in this reading after not keeping in touch with Kym, nor keeping in touch with loved ones on the other side. Automatic handwriting was a bust. Perhaps my spirit guide has written me off as a lost cause.

Yes, I had been preoccupied during those Kym-less months. I'm glad it's over.

Kym (K), Beverly (B), Eleanor (E), and Hal (H)

K: When you said your name, energetically, I got pulled up into a lovely space. Okay Beverly, who would you like to talk to?

B: Mother. Was she with me Saturday when Lynne and I enjoyed looking at Mother's favorite dresses stored in her old steamer trunk?

K: Yes. I see your mom, Eleanor, standing behind you making a heart connection to you both.

B: How nice! I hope it's okay with Mother that I gave her fur coat to Lynne?

K: Eleanor wants to talk about the gift. The fur coat was a joy in her life but it's no longer connected to her. Don't project your hunch that she is still attached to the coat.

E: My dear Bev, I let go of it in love. You can let go of it in love. Whatever you choose to do is okey-dokey to me. Just release it in love.

B: Lynne is thrilled to receive the coat, so it's good to hear Mother's wishes.

K: Even more importantly, you're letting it go to somebody who's going to love it. To Eleanor it's just the progression of her love, your love, and Lynne's love. Sharing love.

B: Lovely. Kym, my current project is to find places where my family artifacts will be appreciated. I initially went through the trunk for a museum, which is organizing an exhibit of old wedding dresses. After looking at the delicate condition of Mother's wedding dress, I decided not to loan it because this museum is not equipped to handle clothing so fragile.

Hunting for a home for mother's stylish fur coat I thought of Lynne, my tall, slender friend who attends the opera. We had the fun of spending hours going through the treasures in Mother's trunk, which included many flapper-era dresses. Serving two different purposes was the goal. One stylish pile to be used for teaching purposes for a fashion school's historic collection, another pristine pile to be offered to museums that collect period clothing. As a drapery historian, I appreciate the educational value of original resources.

K: She has no emotional attachment to any of her clothing now. For other's enjoyment, just pass it on.

B: I'm curious to know how she is these days.

K: Eleanor said she had a lot of healing to do around infants. She helps babies in a hospital by giving them attention. She has a huge smile on her face as she calms them down when they are upset. By helping the infants, she's also healing herself. I don't know why she needs healing, if it's because she had a hard infancy or if motherhood was difficult for her.

B: It could be, but it's hard for me to know. My genealogy research indicates there was family friction that could have influenced her as a baby, and, as a mother, my sister was a colicky baby, which couldn't have been easy.

K: Maybe she had a traumatic birth, whether it was this life or another.

B: Well, I'm not aware of a difficult birth, but she most definitely had a traumatic death if that's a factor!

K: She said no. She's clarifying that it's around births. Remember, we're not only working on our current life problems. We are also working on issues from our past lives at the same time.

[*shocked and surprised*] Oh! She's getting ready to come back!

B: Really? Oh my, I hope it's not too soon! I'm concerned about her being strong enough to take on another life after the tough one she just left. Please tell Mother not to rush. Also, selfishly, I don't want to miss seeing her when I cross over. Oh wait, will her reincarnating prevent me from talking with her through you?

E: Just because I come back to Earth doesn't mean my soul can't connect with you and talk with you. Don't worry, I will be there to meet you when you cross over, whether I'm reincarnated or not. Humans have the wrong perception about the abilities of souls. The idea that souls mimic our human limitations is incorrect. The soul is not affected by the time element. For example, I'm back on Earth as Suzi, and you are still alive as Beverly. As you take your last breath, my soul will know, so the Eleanor part will split from Suzi and come and meet you on the other side.

B: When does this reunion take place? When Suzi's sleeping?

K: Not always, it varies. Usually, each night, in the twilight hours, we leave our bodies and connect with other parts of our soul for further growth. Sometimes it's to visit with others.

B: I sort of understand, but I don't grasp the soul aspect. So much happens that's unseen. I feel like a player in a game, but I don't know what the rules are. I'm just bumbling along!

K: Here's part of why you're bumbling along. Each life has the benefit of forgetfulness which allows us to keep having a unique, new life. This forgetfulness is the blessing and the trap. The blessing part in this new life is that you get to have a fresh start with no memory of past mistakes. Forgetfulness lets you be free to experience something new in a relatively uninhibited way. If we knew all of our past lives and their consequences, we wouldn't play this game as innocently as we do.

The trap part is that you can't learn from your unremembered past mistakes. These consequences of past decisions are still affecting you in covert ways. The challenge is to find out what these issues are, how they play out in your current life, and how to address them.

B: Spot on! I feel like an innocent in this game!

K: And yes, it is definitely a game. We are not given rules, so we haphazardly make our own path to seek out the end result. All moves lead back to God. As we move along this serpentine path, we work through struggles and choices to create a greater version of who we really are. Forgetfulness is the gift to make these new discoveries.

B: The first conversation you and I had was when I discovered Hal had died. Hal was stunned that I was upset. His comment was, "But, you knew." My question is, was I in on the planning stage, or was that just a generalization? Is this another sign of the forgetfulness issue? Can Hal come and answer this?

H: Hi Bev! Yes, to the first question. I was a major player in your life, as you were in mine. Consequently, we both were involved in the planning. We were going to come together on Earth to learn some lessons, then separate and not see each other again until after I died.

K: Bev, I see you sitting at a big table with your mom, dad, sister, Hal, and other major people in your life. All have individual needs. You say, "I really want to come down to Earth and experience …" Someone else responds, "I'd like to experience … Can we help each other on our goals? When will we cross paths? Who's going to take what role? What will the situation be?" It's a mapped out agreement, signed, sealed and delivered! Then you all play your particular roles. It's miraculously organized with little twists and turns. First, we plan it, then promptly forget it, so we can experience it without us knowing when we're on Earth that it was all pre-planned.

After Hal left his form, you were not supposed to be aware he was around you until the next major player crossed your path, which was me. Then you consciously connected with Hal through mediumship to find mutual comfort and support. Your soul knew this, but Beverly on this Earth said, "What? I knew this? If I knew you were going to die so early, I would have prepared myself mentally. If I knew we could still continue our friendship through mediumship or other means, I wouldn't have felt so abandoned and grief-stricken when you died."

B: I've really got that forgetting talent down pat. I had no idea! So what's Hal doing now?

H: Of course, you know I'm in a helping position because that's who I am, a helper.

K: Beverly, since your turbulent exchange with that ghost boy, who was causing you distress but was connected to Hal …

B: Yes! I remember Tim. He was really nasty.

K: Remember, he was mad at Hal. This neighbor boy was in crisis, yet Hal missed seeing the signs he was in trouble. Sometimes people live next door to abusers but don't see what's going on. Apparently, Tim didn't tell Hal of his circumstances. Instead, he felt Hal should have guessed. When the boy died unexpectedly, he didn't cross over into the light due to his intense anger at Hal for not helping him.

H: Beverly, you helped me. Even though you were being attacked by Tim and dealing with all his hostility, you helped my soul to grow through this new knowledge and awareness of this troubled youngster.

B: Isn't that amazing!

H: The last time we talked, I was helping people who were having a crisis of faith. But because of the experience with my former neighbor boy who was disappointed in me, I've now shifted gears and switched to youth in crisis work. Not just faith crisis, but the crisis of abuse. That young boy …

K: … who's standing right next to Hal now! Tim looks so different, he looks so cheerful! OH! I'm going to cry!

B: [*gasping in panic*] Oh, I'm afraid of that guy. I don't want him anywhere near me!

Tim: Ms. Hafemeister, through you, Hal did help me after all. I was able to find you, and in my desperation to get your attention, I chose to be really mean to you. In response to your reaction to my behavior, Hal came to your rescue and found me. [*choking up*]

K: I'm looking at this boy, and I can see how happy he is. He now has so much emotion overwhelming him, he can't speak. Let me tell you the rest of what Tim wants to say, because this is important both for you and for him. First, he wants to apologize. When he was alive, Tim admired Hal but couldn't tell him what was going on in his life. He hoped Hal could figure it out, but he didn't.

Sometimes, people put others on a pedestal. When that person can't live up to the projected hype the admirer built around them, the admirer feels betrayed. Tim pinned his hopes on Hal's keen observation skills. Tim was disappointed, deflated, and desperate. He took those negative feelings with him when he died.

After he died, he was lost in darkness. It was the darkness of his own anger. He was desperate to get out of the world he was locked in. You, Beverly, were his last hope. If you couldn't get Hal to help him, he felt he would have been lost in the abyss forever. You were the conduit to get to Hal.

Second, he's so sorry for what he did to you which opened up Pandora's box. Oh, he's crying. He didn't mean to bring in all those other entities with the pestering voices. They ran in behind him, so he's taking responsibility for opening the lid. He's so desperately sorry, but yet so thankful that you were able to connect him with Hal.

B: [*crying*] That's wonderful! I'm grateful to hear what happened.

K: After Tim crossed over, he and Hal have been with you throughout the process of your recovery.

B: In reclaiming my power over the voices, you mean?

K: Yes, you were never alone. On the other side, Tim's working with Hal in helping other at-risk youth. Tim knows what it's like, the lies kids tell themselves and how they pretend the abuse isn't happening. He's teaching Hal how to help these kids. The two of them are grateful because they're on a new soul path together.

B: I'm so happy it has ended well. Considering what we talked about earlier about all the planning involved, I must have come here knowing this experience was ahead of me?

K: Yes.

B: [*crying*] That makes me feel good and relieves me a lot. I appreciate knowing this. Fellows, may you have great success in your new enterprise!

K: Oh, they're hugging you. The energy of gratefulness and love from this young boy is overwhelming me. I hope you feel this. Let's just be with this a minute. [*whispering*] He's crying and hugging you. Hal is in it, too.

Now they're both stepping back. Hal wants to talk about this alleged mental illness and trip to the hospital which was triggered by Tim opening Pandora's box.

H: Beverly, you are an impetus for many lost souls who, like this young boy, are desperate for help but didn't know how to ask for assistance. They cause havoc and torment, but you need to understand they are simply pleading for help.

K: I'm seeing this vision of you in the dark hospital room. A bright light is emanating out of you. You're the only light source in the room. The rest of the room is midnight blue. Your light is like a magnet to these souls who are ugly beings filled with anxiety and bad behavior trying to hide in the shadows. These gargoyle-like beings act out their angry, vicious words and sounds all around you. You're lying very still in the hospital bed, seemingly oblivious to the fact you're under attack—which you definitely are—by all these souls.

All of a sudden, angels appear around the room to help these yelling, screaming souls hiding in the shadows. Because you were the light ablaze in the bed, the angels could see the beings and cross them over. You were bait to allow the greatest healing for the deepest, darkest, lost souls. That special night, Hal, your parents, and a bunch of other folks, were in the room with you, keeping you corded to Earth so as not to fall into insanity. Without their help, you probably could have gone over the edge.

B: I can well believe that! Before knowing these details, I remember one particular night felt special. Listening to your vision, I believe that evening was what you're referencing. Atypically for a hospital, that night the room was dark except for one bright light attached to the headboard of the bed. For once, the room lighting finally felt homier than a hospital workspace. I told the nurse I liked the light as it was when she came for early evening room check. Unusual for the hospital, there were no other staff interruptions and few sounds along the corridor. As I settled in, a calm voice in my head clearly told me to lay as still as I could as long as I could. I complied without knowing any reasons for the request. It felt right.

Some faint prickly sensations told me something was going on around me, so I did my best to ignore them in order to remain still. At one point I distinctly heard over my left shoulder the comforting nicker of my long departed horse. Yes, horses have unique voices just as people do. In a barn full of horses nickering a welcome at feeding time, I'd always recognize my own horse's greeting. Here he was again, perhaps to comfort me.

The only other animal sensation was that of a struggling bird, probably a crow, who squawked and flopped onto the bed. I overheard two voices having a strange conversation concerning giving me Extreme Unction (Last Rites) and whether it was proper to do it twice in one evening. Being Protestant, the discussion of ceremony had little import for me, though I knew its meaning. I felt fine. Creepy, but fine. Nonetheless, this puzzling event took up most of the night, and I had little sleep. No conscious answers were forthcoming until now, from you.

After that single quiet evening, the rest of the hospital days were filled with the routine bustle of the staff doing medical rounds, coordinating meals, and organizing little activities in an effort to keep the patients as engaged as possible. We were a sorry sight. Most patients slept in their chairs. I kept my socializing to a minimum during the two-week hospital stay. I felt sorry for the organizers and wondered what their attrition rate was.

During this time, I was preoccupied by a fanciful daydream adventure. My private soap opera serial adventure was gruesome but interesting because it was sprinkled with friends. Hal was a frequent participant in the drama. My readily available nonstop experiences consisted of going down into different layers of a huge hell crowded with mostly disheveled, tired people desperately looking for a way to pass to the next higher level. Mostly I relegated this soap opera to being a bizarre time-killer.

K: Beverly, I feel it was more. By what you are saying, could this event have actually happened to you, but you were unaware?

B: All three of these hospital experiences were different, yet eye-opening for me. Even during the hospital check-in process, I knew exactly what my mother must have gone through and the fear she must have felt during her own hospital admission. In many ways I wasn't only living my story but reenacting mother's last terrifying days also. I felt I was ingesting her last days. How shockingly close were our two realities!

K: Was your mom diagnosed as insane?

B: Increasingly over the years, she had become extremely depressed. To see if there was a mental issue causing her depression, mother was admitted to the hospital for observation. Dad told me the experience terrified her, especially when shock therapy was discussed and she saw firsthand the troubled state of the folks she would join. No wonder Mother found an open window outside her fifth floor room and decided to leave unceremoniously. Ironically, her life ended in the mental ward in the hospital while under observation. Her autopsy stated "psychotic depressive reaction," which is a fancy way of saying suicide. One kindness was that no newspaper coverage was made in deference to our desire for private grieving. Dad's pain was particularly profound because he had always been supportive of finding answers to problems. I suspect the stress shortened his life, for he followed her in death three years later.

The first hospital I was taken to had the same policy of allowing people with varying degrees of mental illness severity to co-mingle, if only visually through a window. I was shocked at this stupidity still being practiced many decades after Mother's trauma. How could patients not struggle to keep a positive frame of mind in that atmosphere?

K: It makes sense! I'm seeing your whole family on a soul journey and why you chose to come together. Beverly, you are doing the work your mom was doing, so you have an additional soul connection.

B: Oh, and I have since thought if Mother wanted to latch onto me that if it would help her, it's okay. I've been concerned with her abrupt death and how she is doing now.

K: Beverly, your mom just came forward again.

E: Since you girls have been able to put together these pieces of information, I'm now able to show Kym your story.

K: Beverly, let me describe *the work* your mother is showing me. You're a receptacle for helping other souls. Your mom, Eleanor, was doing the same work as you, but she got lost in her depression. You two played this work out differently. Your mother couldn't take it any longer, couldn't hold onto her will to keep living. This was predestined to happen for both of your souls to grow.

You came into this current life to do her same work, also known as *hell-work*. You were able to take it to the next lower level—go into depression, go into deepest hell daily to help the lost souls, and come back out with your sanity intact.

B: Kym, prior to this conversation, I belittled myself with my doubts. Why couldn't I hang onto my thoughts better by doing what I believe rather than give in to other voices? I berated myself for being so weak and gullible that I could neither stop hearing the voices in my head, nor sift through their requests. I was too apt to relegate my thinking to their demands. In other words, who's in charge of me? I now see it's critical for me to possess strong discernment and self-confidence if I'm to overcome these voices and do the work of helping them.

This business with Tim, which I now realize was real, is one example. I viewed myself as a victim in Tim's frantic, albeit clumsy, effort to get out of his dilemma. Now I hear my role was to be Tim's go-between to Hal. I'm flabbergasted! I thought I was stumbling down my mother's path to mental illness, only to find now it was her unconscious hell-work that caused her demise. To find it was for the beautiful purpose of helping others like Tim is quite a shock! Wonderful, but surprising.

Indeed, I was unwittingly following Mother. Both of us, through lack of knowledge of our hell-work and our attitudinal beliefs, failed to realize that the solution was external not internal! Had we understood we were being approached by lost souls seeking rescue, and had we been less in a self-protection mode, the outcomes for Mother and me would have been less severe. And, maybe less traumatic for the hopeless ones.

K: But you didn't have the rule book. Eleanor didn't either. When you both were on the other side and came up with this scenario, you knew it was going to be a difficult test. By coming to Earth, you had to have forgetfulness so you could live your life experience even while you still did the work, consciously or not. It's a double whammy! In each moment you are trying to find a balance of sanity and normality.

B: [*chuckling*] And I volunteered for this?

K: Just like I volunteered for my mediumship job! I had no need or want to cross over people. I didn't even know it was possible. Timingo just dumps this stuff on me. He said, "Kym, when you go to Savannah, you're going to be crossing over souls." I replied, "What's crossing over souls? Don't you guys do that work? I don't get it."

Beverly, you're unconsciously working with your guide, who's saying, "It's time. We need you to go deep to pull these souls out of hell. You're the vessel, they come to your light." But you don't have a conscious, talking relationship with your guide to know that. Consequently, you felt you innocently slid into something.

In the outline, it was preordained you would do your hell-work by going into the pit of Hades to get these lost souls. Whoever could see your light would be drawn to you. They're angry, hurt beings lost in a pit. They attacked you, like a punching bag, to release their pent-up frustrations. You brought light so the angels could remove them and bring them to the other side, thus ending their suffering. You are the catalyst and the receptacle. From this day forward, you now know what's happening. If it happens again, you need not be scared. You are supported.

B: Oh shoot! Can repeat performances be planned?

K: Maybe you have completed the work you contracted to do, or perhaps the Universe is exposing you to this work in order to answer your questions regarding your mom's problems. This work was also probably a factor to her undiagnosed, ongoing illnesses that baffled her doctors and led to her suicide. I can't pretend to know. Perhaps you don't have to go to the miserable depths of hell again. Maybe you're done.

You have questioned if you're crazy or making these things up. I can completely relate to your dilemma. I too have felt that same way about what I see and hear in my mediumship sessions. Questioning, "Did I make this stuff up? I know people are here, but I don't see them with my human eyes." It's a constant struggle to believe what I'm seeing and hearing. My clients validate the information received from the loved ones as correct, so it helps me to stop doubting myself.

B: I think of my conversations with the psychiatrist. I still go every three months. He's a nice guy who's easy to talk to. On several occasions I've asked him what happened to me. He says he doesn't know. I appreciate his candor, but obviously I'm not going to tell him what you've told me. He won't understand.

K: No, he wouldn't! Here's something similar that might relate to this hell experience; when going to a new event, you feel vulnerable. You watch and figure out what people do, how things work. The next time you go, you're much more confident. You know the game, you know what's cooking.

The guides have given you the detailed knowledge behind your first awake experience in hell. If you're called again, you need not fall into the depths of despair. You now know what is happening and you know the ultimate goal.

Let's stop here to process the information on this topic. I'll call you in a couple of days after we have time to work this out in our heads. The guides tell me your experience will help me teach somebody else. Knowing your example, the next person won't go through as difficult a time as you did. What a great service this will be! It wasn't for naught.

B: I'm glad it might help somebody, but it was tough on me. Actually, I left the hospital feeling worse than when I came. I'm confident people on the other side were helping me when I was home alone, but it was rough.

K: Just know that you're corded to your supporters. They kept you in the Earth plane so you wouldn't lose your mind.

B: With all the haranguing, I still felt I got close to that stage.

K: Since your mom took the suicide road, she was your greatest corder of support for you not to leave.

E: Beverly, you had to stay, you had work to finish! I didn't want you to check out too soon because you were the light. If death had snuffed out your light, like I did mine, those souls couldn't have been rescued.

K: Have you ever seen the movie, *What Dreams May Come*, starring Robin Williams? The guides keep flashing this reference to me. This symbolic story was about a depressed wife who, through grief and loss, fell into a dark pit of hell. Her husband, in order to rescue her, had to row a boat through a deep, black lake sardine-packed with naked people frantically flailing their arms and legs, crying and screaming for his help. Anxious and worried that he would not be able to row to his wife, he was in great peril of being engulfed by the howling masses, and afraid he would topple into the jet-black waters below.

This scene is a visual representation of what happened to you in the hospital. You both were on a quest. Yours was unconscious. His was conscious. You were in a bed. He was in a boat. You both were crossing into different dimensions. Your desperate, lost souls were like gargoyles. His were a tangle of naked humans. You were overloaded with voices that triggered your fear of tipping into insanity. He was vulnerable with his concern of reaching his wife, which was overshadowed by his panic of being pitched into the wildly lashing waves. You believed the voices were screaming at you, when actually, they were screaming to you for help like the people who were grabbing at the movie husband. Your goal was to help these gargoyle souls, his was to save his wife. You both accomplished your quest.

What stopped you from tipping into mental illness? First and foremost, it was your internal strength. I want you to take credit for that success. But it was also the cording of your parents, Hal, and other people who kept you anchored. You couldn't help the lost ones if you joined them!

B: That's scary! I didn't see the movie, but I saw the advertising promo featuring that boat scene clip. It was so upsetting graphically, I quickly flipped channels. Little did I know I was going to run into a similar situation!

K: Isn't it amazing how the Universe weaves these signs for us to understand at a later time?

B: In Mother's case, her hospital wasn't as helpful as it could have been.

K: You and your mom were working similar spiritual journeys. It wasn't a physical journey in the way a hospital could mend a leg. You both were spiritually attacked while on a mission to help souls. Eleanor didn't have enough support to be able to come out the other end. In her vulnerability, these troubled entities kept sucking on her light. I do believe she helped many, but over the long haul the work physically depleted her.

When you both mapped this outline, she decided she would go first and fall. She had to die so that you would take up the baton and fulfill it for both of you. Had she remained here, sickly in her body, her help would be limited and her pain great. Her choice was to be on the other side to anchor your cord connection and act as your advocate through perilous events. These were the choices you both made to do your job, to accomplish your task, and progress on your soul journeys by helping all concerned. Everything is connected. We are all one.

Well, this has been a full session. Let's stop here.

B: I'm fine with that, there is a lot to process on these topics. Thanks, everyone, for all the help today.

Beverly's Personal Journey:

Emotionally, two people particularly touched me in this reading. The first person is my mother. The more I know of her life, the more in awe of her I am. She and her generation were quite familiar with trauma. She witnessed World War I as a child, skimped during the Great Depression as a young wife with two babies, and participated in World War II by doing her version of Rosie the Riveter. An outline like that would be more than sufficient for the average person. Now, with the uncovering of Mom's hell-work, it is unsettling to picture her consciously confronting visions of troubled people desperate for her help. Being stalked is a life filled with a heavy burden. How did she have the energy to keep our family of four up and happily running? I am truly stunned by her lifetime accomplishment.

On a different note, I wanted to mention how comforted I was by Mother's explanation of that special event in the two weeks hospital stay with the crossing of the gargoyles. It really helped me to make sense of why I was there.

Additionally, in the same stay, I inhabited a vision of what I thought was a soap opera adventure but was actually a functioning hell society. I was witnessing a hell nation of self-imposed souls, built in layers, not unlike Dante's *Divine Comedy*. In this vision, hell's many levels had been opened to me. At the lowest level I could hear the sounds of shoveling announcing a deeper, more depressing area that was being excavated for future, solitary residents. Stationed slightly above the new area, the farm folks labored. They and their gaunt horses worked hard in the dark grime to eke out a living. The higher levels, while visually lighter, were at all times covered with a dirty haze of suspended dust. Living there was more foreboding because of the cunning, backstabbing behavior of the status-seeking occupants. Each level had its own crummy political order, hierarchy, and power plays which were constantly being played out.

Many times I was terrified for my safety, being thrust into a society who had little respect for its members. People were to be used and discarded after they had served their purpose. Carnal self-interest was supreme. Inflicting pain on others was the norm in this society, but offended me sufficiently so that I locked some events out of my memory bank. I felt stuck in this game and wanted my life back.

Was the hell nation also part of my yet unknown work? Were Mother and I connected down there too? Hearing the terms *the work* and *hell-work* in reference to both my mother and me, increasingly feels like it's of major significance in my journey. If I want answers, I've got to be more of an instigator. In fact, I must be willing to spend a little time questioning, researching, comparing, hypothesizing, and examining. Initiative seems to be a requirement, but fear gets in my way.

The second person who touched me profoundly by his growth, was Tim. I didn't understand the significance of him inadvertently opening me up to a bunch of people, until I read the adventure of Kym and Hemmy with the belief clusters. Apparently, Tim was locked in his world of darkness as a soul fragment with a big wedge filled with hatred directed at others. When one of the magnetic red ball core beliefs clusters floated by, Tim's wedge of hatred clamped on, thus he was trapped by his own belief system. Now I'm putting all of these things together.

By the time he found me, Tim entered my aura not fully aware he was dragging in other soul fragments with the same mindset and attitude of his belief cluster. To speculate further, I think our human need for social bonding is part of the magnetic energy at the core of these clusters, which strengthens the power of the connection. Like attracts like.

Tim's growth was demonstrated with his assistance in cording me. It sounds like he's experiencing an apprenticeship with on-the-job training to see how hell-work affects people. It's gratifying to see Tim is helping me.

On the lighter side, the update with Hal's activities lets me know the decision making abilities on the other side are fluid. When he saw a need for young people like Tim to be helped, Hal could volunteer. It tells me crossed-over spirits can change jobs according to their interests. They have growth opportunities as their interests expand.

Kym's Professional Journey:

When Beverly shows concern about her mother's return to a new incarnation, Eleanor told us that even though she returned to an Earth life, she can still talk to Beverly, meet her, and will be there when Beverly crosses over. Eleanor is still linked to Beverly.

This new aspect, we're calling *twilight links*, are like out-of-body events. It's specifically where a living soul can link up with other souls on Earth and in different levels of evolution. We tend to forget that we are divine beings even when we are in the human form.

As human beings in our sleep, we are freed from our bodies so our divine selves can perform a variety of actions. We can rush to loved ones who are struggling with problems, we can hook up with our deceased ancestors and family, we can visit, in dreams of long ago, friends and most importantly, we can call on others for help (live family or friends).

I can't count the times I have had someone visit me in my sleep; old loves showing up to ask for help or to chat. My current and old friends have found their way to me when I was feeling low or needing kindness. Aside from all the dead people who visit me in the night, which is often, I'm equally touched by people that are still alive who pop in for some quality time. Even my clients reach out to me in nightly visits for comfort.

Many times in the morning after one of these twilight links, I'll reach out to these living night visitors, through a phone call or an email. Some think I'm mad when I ask, "Do you need to talk?" even though I haven't spoken to them in many years. They either say, "How did you know?" or "This is so weird, you've been on my mind for a few days," or I just get a simple "??" in an email reply. I'm aware of these links happening and I want to acknowledge the visit, even if to them I come off as a bit wacky. My ability to realize that people visit is not due to my psychic skills. We all have this skill, but I'm conscious of these happenings because I'm paying attention and not writing it off as a fluke or as a wandering mind.

Later in the session, things started to get very heavy for us. I got very clear visions of an experience Beverly had in the hospital. This vision fell into that *uncomfortable* realm for me, since I have never been one to watch scary movies. It put the hair on my arms on end. But I had to keep from projecting my feelings onto the interpretation of the vision in order to not scare Bev. Remaining calm is one of the hard parts of what I do with this work. I'm told all kinds of things that make me question and stretch my own limited beliefs. I'm seeing it, feeling it, hearing it, and engaging with it, how can I doubt it? Yet, many times I struggle and I have to work through it in my own processing.

The entire exchange was wild! Beverly was helping to cross over scary looking spirits caught in hell. That made me question some of my own thoughts around the topic of a hell. I was taught that in hell we are damned. I never really believed in a hell. Now I'm being shown and told there *is* a hell. What the hell?

As things go on, I'm stumped as to why a human is needed to help cross over the souls in hell? Why Beverly and Eleanor? Aren't there other more trained spirits used in this work than these poor uneducated humans?

I was saddened and frightened by what Eleanor had to go through as a human doing this hell-work. What a difficult assignment. My heart broke for her journey and her terrifying demise. I fully connected to Beverly, to commit to helping her in any way I could. I was not going to let Beverly get lost in her hell-work like her mother did.

This invisible structure is getting more and more complex as we work through these sessions. Not only do we have twilight link with souls, but some of us go to work on saving souls in hell. I'm shocked and intrigued, even if it sounds more fictional as we go along.

When the guides used the *What Dreams May Come* imagery, I was gobsmacked! I saw the movie once and I had no idea what 85% of it was talking about! Seeing the visual with the guides' interpretation of the similarities to Beverly's work in hell, it made many parts of the movie fall into place for me.

Eleanor continued to tell us that her work and Beverly's work was laid out in the outline they developed prior to this life. My first thought was, "What were they thinking? Were they both high?" What would possess them to choose to have their sanity tested? Was this job so important that the little sanity tidbit was too small to deter them?

My take away is that, as divine humans, we are not only having a typical outlined life experience on Earth. Some of us are also doing additional work during our down time of sleep, and this work seems to be very connected to the other levels of existence. How many other jobs do we humans do in our sleep to help the other levels?

After the heaviness of this session, we hoped that the next session, which was to take place a few weeks later, would lead into lighter topics. But sadly, it too leads to more events fraught with fear.

Personal Growth Questions:

1. In reference to twilight links, how do you feel about leaving your body during sleep? Are you fearful, grateful, or something else?
2. Do you consider ignorance of past lives a blessing, a curse, or both?
3. Does it help you to get into the flow of your life's purpose to know life isn't random because you sat around that table on the other side planning this life? Why?

Walking Life's Balance Beam

February 1, 2013, Beverly Mindset

The last session dealt with some far-out situations, so I'm looking for some simple, practical applications today. Some questions came up about my impact on the world, and I wanted Hal's input based on his experiences.

Beverly (B), Kym (K), Timingo (T), Hal (H), Eleanor (E), and Ray (R)

B: Kym, I would like to start with my former minister, Hal, to see what he thinks of the church I lovingly attend. The bothersome philosophical issue I don't hear the congregation address is whether or not to help stuck, unmotivated individuals. Either I'm not hearing it or it's not there.

My church is very strong about everyone leading their own life, "You're my brother and you're an adult, so you can figure out life on your own," but in cases of shame, abuse, pride, depression, illness, dementia, physical limitations, age factors, or poverty, am I not encouraged to be a conduit for assistance? Will I be taking over and making choices for them? In this scenario, they could become dependent, or, if they are young, they might not develop a backbone if I think for them.

H: Beverly, you have the right balance. You have what seems like a conflict, but it's really not. There are boundaries on both sides. In my profession as a minister, I would look to my brother and say, "How can I help you?" If people don't want your help, you need to step back and let them take their own action. But sometimes they accept your offer, and then you can help them along.

Bev, you have the clarity of understanding that there *is* a fine line. You are in an educational situation at your church, which you value because you can relate to both sides of most issues, yet others do not see both sides. You need to bring in the other aspect so it's not one-sided! Balance needs to happen. This is an opportunity for you to have an impact if you choose to share.

Sometimes people aren't aware of an opportunity in front of them. Sometimes they don't even know what they really want. We can help them see their opportunities, see their possibilities. Open their minds to how they can use their talents and skills to advance themselves. That's how we're our brother's keeper. Unfortunately, churches are notorious for having extremes. They buy into a doctrine and follow it to their detriment. Instead, churches can be a support or bridge between two extremes.

B: I have a tendency in group functions to sit there and fail to interject my opinions, so my ideas slide off of me unspoken. Sometimes I reprimand myself the next day, knowing I kept my mouth shut when I had something to offer. When I do interrupt, it's mostly when people are being too "Pollyanna-ish." Consequently, many people think I'm being negative when I'm really advocating a thorough examination of both sides, be it positive or negative.

H: Bev, you're always at the brink of an internal struggle. Your pattern is whether or not to take the opportunity to add to the discussion. Either take the opportunity or give it up! Bosom Buddy, quit having these self-abusive internal struggles! You have years on you, wisdom on you, life experience on you, and you have a wealth of knowledge to bring to this church to open up their minds. They don't have all the answers. They need your input for greater insight to find the answers.

B: You've just given me a perfect example of why I treasure your advice. You get right to the heart of the matter. Thanks.

Speaking of balance, my dad Ray was the perfect role model for me. Kym, may I hear what Dad has to say? He probably knows I gave his YMCA memorabilia to a couple historical societies. I hope he approves.

K: Yes, he's happy the photographs, yearbooks, and ephemera will be seen, studied, and enjoyed by others, like your mom and her period wardrobe. Both of your parents have a good attitude about enjoying artifacts during their lives without unhealthy attachment.

R: I'm so proud of you.

B: Oh … [*crying*] I'm proud of you too.

R: You have been through such a releasing at this stage of your life by allowing things to leave your sphere as a means of releasing grief, to help others, and be a joy to them. In that letting go of things in the grief process, there is great loss and great courage you're showing. I'm proud of you and your bravery. You are a courageous girl. These last few years have been fraught with enormous challenges and you have faced them all. Your work with desperate souls has and will be your legacy of courage.

B: That's ironic! I've never particularly thought of myself as a courageous person living my everyday life.

K: Well, I see you totally as a courageous person after all you have gone through. I don't know if I could have done it. Even in my horrible times, learning to help souls when they were still making me physically ill, I didn't go to the depths you did.

B: If courageousness is a positive personality trait, on the flip side, my emotional idealistic enthusiasm gets me into trouble. When I get involved in a project before I have thought it through, I say, "Yeah, I'll do that," but soon I think, "Good grief! What have I gotten myself into?" Proof of my enthusiasm is signing on to help souls without thinking through the challenges I would have to face to accomplish the goal.

K: You and I do the same thing. We get excited about new experiences. Once, Timingo took me to my recent *Life Between Life Review*, which is a period of time after my death from one life and before I go into the next life. It's the time of review and reflection. My last life in the Middle East as a man was reviewed before I came into this Kym life. As I expected, we looked at how the life affected me and my family. To my surprise, many other levels were studied with the counsel of a series of individual wisemen. At each level we reviewed with a specific perspective how my Middle East life impacted my community, my state, my country, and the whole of humanity. On the tippy-top level we discussed with council when and if I was going to reincarnate into a next Earth life. When Timingo and I arrived, the wiseman said, "You again! Don't you ever take a rest?" My reply was, "No, it's too exciting. Let's go back down!"

See, you're doing the same thing Beverly. You've got courage, and you keep coming back to give yourself a wider perspective. On the other side, you and your spirit guide review and analyze your past experiences with thoughtful advisers concerning your next best options when planning to return to Earth. In writing your new outline, one of the pleasant choices you made was to say, "I'm going to plant some clues and opportunities to remind me of my goals, so I'm not confused and blown away when the going gets tough."

T: We knew coming into your sphere of understanding was going to be challenging. You needed anchors to ground you and hold you steady along the way. We're pleased you picked up on many of these clues once in the body.

B: So I left myself clues? … Oh! Wait a minute. I remember a friend suggested the book by Jim Marion which I read before I started having my problems. As the memoir turned out, this mystic had life experiences roughly similar to mine. Having read about his trials helped fortify me during my own bleakest moments and bucked me up. Did I send that to myself?

K: Yes, your exposure to that book through a friend was one of these little clues you sent to yourself to help you cope in this life. Likewise, you put me in your sphere to have somebody to talk to about connecting the dots. Everything is planned for our greater growth. You're an advanced soul who came to do some advanced experiencing to get closer to your God-self. You're being opened up to very high-level knowings.

E: Yes Beverly, Kym is correct. You're coming closer to your God-self, which knows all of it. Allow your own knowing to come in. Trust yourself. Follow these steps. Look at your perceived problems, pause a minute. Don't be afraid, but think to ask yourself, "What would be the best action to take?"

B: Thanks for your encouragement to keep plugging away at my challenges. Therefore, it will be no surprise to you that I still would like to know more about the strange night when I swear an angry bird crashed onto my hospital bed. I didn't see anything, but I sensed it was a crow. What was that all about?

T: A bird's soul journey has the possibility of being trapped in hell. Birds have beliefs much like humans do. Unseen and unheard by you, the twisted human souls growling and hissing in your darkened room were imprisoned in their own hell just as the bird was that evening.

B: I'm glad I didn't see any of that scene as originally described by Kym and now by you. Frankly, I'm only starting to get the significance of that evening and assume more will unfold for me as my thoughts mature.

As for the birds on a soul journey of their own, now that's an important paradigm shift! Any perceptive person working with animals recognizes they have personality traits, but you're saying it's deeper. I'll refrain from going through that door at this moment, but I'll return at another time to investigate animal life.

Instead, let me talk about the aftermath of my most recent, third hospital experience. Getting out of bed one morning after my two week confinement, I heard sounds in my head that started to blot out the more or less continuous voices. I didn't consider it music because it was not pleasant. These sounds were ugly, spooky noises in my head and they began to gain strength and intensity like a chant. I didn't like the low-pitched racket and told myself to shut it down. I couldn't! I tried harder for many minutes without luck. What was happening to me?

I ran into the bathroom to look into the mirror and was shocked to see my pathetic face. I looked thin, gray, and drawn. My eyes were dark and deeply set. My hair was sparse, stringy, and dirty. Alarmed, I picked up the hand mirror so I could see the back of my head. Indeed, my hair was so scarce I could see large rows of my scalp as if some bird's claw had combed my head from top to bottom. All the while the hypnotic, ugly chant was in my head! It wouldn't stop!

I focused on the now undulating sounds in an effort to stop them. Time went by without result. Prayers, increasingly fervent, had no immediate effect. I felt I was falling into an insanity I could not escape with the combination of voices and ugly sounds. I had reached the bottom of hopeless disempowerment. What if I would never experience quiet again? I dragged myself back to bed in deep despair. What happened to me?

K: Let me see if I understand your panic. You looked in the mirror and were alarmed to see your apparent sudden hair loss. You thought the chants were putting a hex on you that included hair loss?

I'm asking the guides. I don't feel it was a hex. It was a healing. I feel souls gathered around you, their energy shooting around you is positive.

Remember, we are having a human experience, too. Medicine and other things could be causing the hair problem. However, I have a feeling the reason you're having hair loss is a result of the work you did in hell, not from the chanting. The souls doing the chanting tried to heal you. I feel all love and help. I don't feel it was to harm you, it was to help you.

T: We're showing Kym a vision of a person who's been mugged so she can identify with your plight. You felt mugged by the onslaught of voices and loss of personal control. It put you in an extremely fearful state. In your fragile condition, when help came, you perceived the chanting as another attack. We were sending you healing music through voice chants. We were conspiring to help you, not hurt you. Your reaction to the chanting caused more panic because you thought more malevolent voices had arrived. Your fear was understandable. Beverly, you didn't realize there are lots of voices there to support you. You reacted with fear, which became a wall between you and the healing. You need to see the energy variations in their voices, like Kym does. Learn to perceive the differences.

K: I see dead people all the time. For instance, your mother, father, and Hal are standing before me now—they are crossed spirits. But a week ago, three young kids showed up and started talking to me. It took a while to catch on that the kids were ghosts, not crossed-over spirits. I have had to learn to perceive which ones are ghosts and which ones are crossed-over spirits. It's such a fine, fine line. There is a distinct difference. I do this by focusing on their energy, then sensing how they feel.

You have to do the same detective work. Listen to the nuances. The first thing you need to do is decide if its negative. If they're telling you to do something wrong or bad, you can put them in the realm of "not good." If they're just talking to you, giving you information, or chanting, you have to allow your body to sense them without fear jumping up and clamping the door shut. Fine-tune your senses in order to know what their motive is for visiting.

B: Yes, you're right. Calming myself down to sort them out is something I must master … yet that's when I'm at my most vulnerable. It's important to figure out what these visitors want and why they presented themselves.

Unfortunately, I've got a hair trigger when it comes to scary surprises, and I jump into flight mode instinctively. The odd thing is, I can't think of why in this lifetime I should be susceptible to sudden foreboding. But I do remember that even as a kid, I couldn't watch scary movies. Now I see that fright, carried over into adulthood, cramps my style in achieving what I want. Have you run into that trait before, Kym?

K: My client Stella, an untrained natural medium from birth, was aware she could see her dead loved ones, but she freaked out if any random dead strangers came to her for help. She would cry out, "Go away! I only want to talk to dead people I know!" She was so scared that she couldn't sleep for months on end. That's when she sought me out. After I explained the needs of these strangers and her part in helping them on their soul journey, she calmed down, but she was still wary.

A few nights later, after our session, Stella's guides devised a plan and enlisted her trusted, dead former boyfriend, to help her. He brought an unknown, deceased child to her. The boyfriend knew Stella had the biggest heart in the world for children. As expected, she helped the child cross over, and when nothing bad happened from that crossing, it helped heal Stella's resistance to strangers. Now she crosses over people all the time with no fear. The guides know how to help us get over our hurdles so we can start our spiritual work!

It's the same thing with you. You have the ability to hear and to help souls. You have direct access now to those souls in their personal hells. Your exposure to this work with the voices and the mental disturbances in the hospital was a hard road. You don't have to do that anymore. Take the easy road. Sleep. Sleep will allow your soul to do its work without the drama trauma interrupting your daily life.

Say to yourself, "I can do this in my sleep, which helps others and helps me because I feel healthy, happy, and more in control of my emotions." When you go to bed at night, have a little ritual. Call in everybody to cord your physical body to Earth. Announce to the Universe, "If I need to work tonight, just give me a call, but in the meantime, my body needs sleep."

[*laughing*] Say to your crossed-over spirit team, "Okay, everybody, get in bed with me so we're ready to go if we're needed. I want to do the work my soul needs to do and be there for others. I want to continue the work, but I don't want this to harm me physically. I'm going to sleep now knowing I'm safe. I trust you to keep watch while I'm asleep."

B: Yes, I confess my resistance comes from my fear of getting into situations where I'm alone, stranded and vulnerable, so I tend not to want to venture out.

T: It's highly orchestrated. You've never been alone on this journey. You could never say, "Okay I'm here. Where is everybody else?" [*laughing*]

B: How does the team know to be on duty to receive souls?

K: Everybody knows what's going on. You haven't known in the past, but you are getting inklings of what's going on now. You may not always go to the deep darkest hell, you might go elsewhere. Beverly, be open to where you're needed.

That's how I look at my work with ghosts. If I'm at the grocery store and some ghost needs crossing, all right, I'll stop what I'm doing to cross him. Spirits are everywhere. You and I are human beacons of light whether we are in a movie theater, in a church, walking down the street, or anywhere.

B: But why do they need me? I don't understand.

K: I also asked this same question of Timingo, "Why do you need a short, fat, fifty-four-year-old woman in Cleveland to cross ghosts over? Why me?" I still don't really know why except to know I'm a vital component of this work just as you are. I'm sure they'll tell us the answer when the time is right.

T: Kym, remember I told you, we are doing this work as a team, and there are certain souls who need you specifically. It's the same for Beverly.

Beverly, in your case, in a past life as the sorceress you developed great power as a protector. This advanced power is why you now can go to the depths of hell even though you have a different personality than the sorceress. Not all humans have that ability.

K: That's a new thought! One thing I know for sure is we didn't get as wise as we are in just one lifetime. It's all piggy backed on from life to life, just as you have with the sorceress. As souls, we want to learn, experience, and grow, so we have multiple lives by coming back down to Earth. This time, however, once I leave the Kym life, I want a million years off! I'm tired!

B: Believe me, I share that sentiment! But seriously, how does anyone come back to their awareness of all-knowing?

K: Each lifetime we develop skills depending on what we're drawn to as a profession. We don't lose these skills when we die. They become part of our toolbox that might remain dormant in the next life, but if needed the skills could be activated in this new life. Then when this new skill shows up, we call it a natural ability, not realizing it wasn't natural at all. We sweated over developing this skill in a past life!

For example, one day in my current life, an Earth spirit, Daniel, showed up demanding, "You need to write a song, both lyrics and music." I replied, "What are you talking about? I don't know how." He insisted, "But you must! The words you will compose will heal in ways you have not yet expressed." I questioned who he was. His response was, "I am the herald of the music in the wind. I'm not the wind but the music in it. I need you to write the lyrics and melody. When it's done, I'll broadcast it in the wind. It will stir people back into harmony! And you already agreed to do it!"

Seemingly, I agree to everything when I'm on the other side! That bossy guy nagged me for two months until, finally, I wrote lyrics to two songs. Once I gave them to him, I never saw him again. The point is we have talents in more ways than our current life indicates. Many are hidden. Your hidden talents like writing, singing, and painting are for you, but will benefit others too. We send ourselves clues like books, videos, opportunities, and pivotal people to cross your path to trigger these hidden talents to come to the surface.

For example, one may write a song to express an internal need, but once written it goes on to be a clue or message for another. You have to be in the moment to allow the dormant talents to come awake in you and then be given from you to others, like my two wind songs. Information given to us now might not be used until years later. Many seeds take a long time before they are ready to germinate. For instance, your mother planted a seed as to what your work would be, but you, Beverly, don't remember it. However, your soul said, "In my new life as Beverly, my mom will die first and the seed my mom planted will take forty years to germinate until I become consciously aware of the agreement from the other side to work in hell."

T: We really want you, Beverly, to release this fear, this holding of your breath that you're doing around this work. Our connection is not clear to you because of your fear.

K: I feel your fear in your body, like a vise around your heart and chest area. You're afraid of the voices and falling back into Crazyville.

E: Look, Daughter, you're going to create your reality if you don't stop it!

K: Bev, your mother meant it! It reminds me of a story about a man and woman who had been married forty years. Every night the startled woman woke up saying, "Honey, wake up! Somebody's downstairs." Dutifully, the husband got up every evening and went downstairs to check things out. Nobody was there. He went back to bed.

One night the wife wakes up again and says, "I know somebody's downstairs!" He walks downstairs to face the barrel of a stranger's gun and the words, "Give me all your valuables." The husband complies. When the robber turns to leave, the husband shouts, "Wait! Wait! Where are you going?" "I'm leaving!" "No you're not! You go upstairs and show yourself to my wife because she's been waiting for you for forty years!" I love that story! But see, the wife created her reality by waiting for the robber to show up. She willed him to her.

T: Beverly, don't create your reality! Start breathing, release this fear around your situation. You can't hear the difference between a soul wanting your help and one trying to help you until you relax enough to hear the fine line between them.

E: Just breathe, relax into it, and allow your senses to do their job. You now know the work, you're not alone.

K: Eleanor's being very strong here. Use the tools you didn't know you had when this all started. You don't personally have to connect emotionally to the happenings down in the bowels of hell. You can do your work, but not to the point where it hurts you.

Okay Bev, you like to reason. Close your eyes and picture your fear. What color is it? What do you see? Describe it.

B: [*pausing*] A big, cold, icy blue block.

K: Okay, now keep looking at that icy block and watch what happens. Say to the cube, "I am strong enough, wise enough, and I have tons of help." What's happening to the block?

B: I saw a friendly sun come out, the icy blue block melted, and I'm standing in a puddle! I didn't realize I was inside of the block!

K: Yes, the fear had enveloped you! Now visualize all these gold cords going to you from your parents, friends, and God. Note that I'm holding a cord too. You have the tools to keep you safely here. You don't have to walk to the edge of the cliff anymore. Just be a human beacon in your daily life; and when you go to sleep, you will be fulfilling your life mission.

B: Change isn't always easy.

K: Say to yourself, "I know I have decided a long time ago what my beliefs are about, how the world works and functions. Now as an adult I'm finding the world is much bigger than I first imagined. I'm open to reevaluate what I have previously decided." Change doesn't have to be scary, especially since the gifts of free will and free choice is always available to us.

If there are no other questions, remember I'm always at the other end of the phone. Think this over. Listen to the recording. There's so much information here, I know you'll process it intellectually, but give your soul time to process it too. The biggest message today is, breathe and bring that fear wall down.

In closing, I'm so grateful for you calling and allowing me to channel this new information. By allowing me in on your journey, I'm learning too.

B: I thank all the assembled people and you, Kym, for your curiosity and great talent!

Beverly's Personal Journey:

I couldn't wait to get home after my third confinement! Surely my life would be better. But alas, it wasn't. In fact, the negative voices got stronger, more taunting, and rudely demanding. I tried appeasement by complying when the voices told me to get rid of all of my automatic handwriting correspondences. Into the dumpster those papers went. Okay, so go away now, guys!

"No. Now throw away any other evidence you have of Hal." Well, that order sent me into a tizzy of additional internal conflict. Yes, I felt I was still clinging to Hal. Grief is not a good thing. I needed to liberate him. I scurried around the house to ferret out Hal's mementos to destroy. I thought back to my guilt over my failed attempt with the Osage orange fruit planting in the back yard. This purging was the extreme opposite to Kym's first reading of the loving release of grief. This violent purging was a lousy substitute.

During the intervening months, if I listened carefully, I could sometimes bring forward from the pack of voices a kind, patient voice. This voice was always there with encouraging words and positive answers when the bullying voices accosted me with words insisting that I was not a person "worthy of being alive." My unidentified supportive voice was repeatedly called upon as I weakened. My ego pride had fled long ago.

During my hospital confinements, I remember lying in bed at night listening to the nightly moans and ramblings of patients in my hospital wing. Some folks gave vent to living in a hellish location in their minds. Alarmed for them instead of being concerned for myself, I immediately sent them healing thoughts of well-being and calm. Gratefully, I never lapsed into a stage of my own personal hell. In these times, my mind went to my mother and her struggles. I have no idea how it had been for her back then. Due to the distance, I was never able to visit her, but I know the sad result. She and I, decades apart, shared the same concern. Mother lost her grip and she chose to escape her tormentors. With me, I struggled not to make that same choice. We both simply wanted help.

After returning back home one gloomy day, I was so beaten down by the constant nagging negative voices in my head that I got in my car and slowly drove to the hospital, debating all the way with myself about the wisdom of my intention to re-enter the hospital system for the fourth time. Fortunately, I parked in the wrong place in the ambulance lot, walked in the wrong entrance, and stood by the door timidly watching a woman working at her desk, who seemed to deliberately look at me, but did not respond or call to me. I was in the ambulance emergency entrance, the wrong location. At the time I debated afresh in my mind, "Should I or shouldn't I turn myself in?" Knowing that three stays in the hospital hadn't helped me, why would a fourth work? Everything about this was wrong! I made the decision to turn around slowly and quietly tiptoe back to my car, and go home alone. I realized the standard medical treatment was not my route to a cure.

I get chills thinking about how close I came to making the wrong decision. Help outside the mainstream was my best hope. Now I'm having a flashback of Kym telling me I had been hospitalized in past lives, too. In earlier times they were called insane asylums. Not a pretty picture. I tend to think she's right. No wonder I turn cold at the thought of such a life.

All this activity took place before I had assimilated the importance of the sorceress life and her mission to stop running away and regain her power. If I had understood earlier that it was my job to find my power, I might have hung on longer and firmer to overcome the harassment of my voices. In hindsight, the guides probably gave me all the hints and clues through these readings that they could. The key cause for the sorceress's downfall has not yet been discovered, but her decision to reject her talent and become helpless speaks volumes about self-loathing.

Now, I'm learning to speak up for myself, my mother, and others. We need to find multiple avenues of help for folks hearing disruptive voices in their head. Labeling them with the catch-all phrase of mental illness is not the answer. Part of my journey is about identifying and removing negative energy that influences and masquerades as mental illness. The symptoms presented to a professional may look the same, but the treatment is not.

It's time to review the tenets of the professionals, not to be more timid, but to open minds beyond traditions. From my experience, I request the medical profession specializing in the care and treatment of people displaying what are labeled as mental illnesses to broaden their professional viewpoints by learning about past lives and their impact on current lives. Those courageous medical people willing to collaborate with serious professional teachers in the alternative treatment communities need to exchange freely their findings with one another. Both hold vital keys to healing their charges, but only if they start swapping information and respecting each other's hands-on experiences.

Kym's Professional Journey:

Early in the session, I share the Life Between Life experience I had after leaving my last incarnation in the Middle East, prior to my Kym life.

Many people believe that after we die God will make some sort of judgment upon us as to how we lived our life. When Timingo took me to this review, I was gobsmacked as to the lack of judgment attached to the experience. As we reviewed every detail of the life, every look and feeling of each person I interacted with, Timingo and I discussed it in great detail, but without one ounce of judgment.

With each review of the wisemen, the entire experience was done with no emotional guilt or regret, without seeing anything as good or bad. It was just an experience to come into my awareness.

This, it seems to me, is one more part of the invisible structure that happens after each and every lifetime. It's reviewed in love, kindness, and awareness of each moment.

The rest of this session brings us back to a topic we have discussed already, but it's worth repeating. Discernment is the number one skill all humans need to fine-tune. Discernment in the human experience is needed in two different stages.

The first stage is a quick evaluation or judgment about something or someone. In our everyday life, we all need to be discerning. Is this man or woman the type of person I want in my life, whether as a friend, as a romantic interest, or as a business partner? Is that friend really a friend, or a foe in disguise? Is this job better than another?

The second stage of discernment is looking at our first reaction and moving past the initial review—and the emotions triggered—to see the situation or person more clearly in order to determine if the first assessment is still how you feel. This second stage of discernment is not always done by people. They tend to stay with their first assessment. They don't revisit it to see if it's still true, which is a disservice to themselves and to those they have judged one way or another.

Discernment is important in our regular life, but even more so in our spiritual awakening. In Beverly's case, and in the life of other "sensitives" who hear voices, come into contact with ghosts, or see visions, discernment is the only way out of fear.

When a client calls and says, "I have something in my house. I think it's a demonic entity," I get annoyed because it's the *first place* they go in assessing the situation. I blame the media for planting fear in the minds of the audience. In the last 15 years as a professional in this field, I have never come across a demonic being.

With spirits, be it ghosts or souls in their own hell, I have never found them to be innately *evil*. Some are souls acting out bad behavior due to their ignorance, fear, and pain. As in our human life, we run across people all the time who choose bad behavior to get what they want. When they die and find themselves in a hell situation or on the ghost plane, the bad behavior doesn't change, as we saw with the spirit of Tim.

Regardless of how souls choose to behave, a sensitive like Beverly needs to be able to sort through the actions and get to the reason why they have come to her. It's why discernment is one of the most important skills I teach to anyone who is hearing voices, seeing disturbing visions, or sensing ghosts around them. Falling into fear is what makes this type of psychic awakening more difficult than it has to be. Ignorance fuels fear.

As I walked through the times I was afraid, it was always because I didn't understand or know why something was happening. Yet, when I learned more facts, I could move out of fear. I heard a wonderful quote the other day, but I'm not sure who to credit. It was, "Fear is just the lack of information." These simple words are true. Think about it.

In the next chapter, life gets very interesting because it's the first time Beverly and I met personally. No surprise, the teachings kept happening!

Personal Development Questions:

1. What's been the primary pattern in your life about being your brother's keeper? How do you feel about your actions concerning others? How would you change your behavior?
2. Have you noticed how letting go of physical items like old family trinkets is similar to releasing energy? Think back to something you had a long time but had to get rid of. After the initial sting of the loss, did you feel freer? Less weighed down?
3. What are your thoughts regarding the Life Between Life review story?

Good Grief! I'm Running a Ghostly Boarding House!

April 27, 2013, Kym's Mindset

Beverly and I share an interest in the work of the A.R.E. (Association for Research and Enlightenment), the Edgar Cayce Foundation, which is where Bev had seen me talk back in 2009. When the grandson of Edgar Cayce was doing a talk in Kentucky, my friend Mary and I decided to attend, and Beverly offered to put us up for the conference weekend. Up until this time, Beverly and I had never met in person, so I was excited to put a face to the voice.

As Mary and I drove into the driveway, we arrived to find the 70 plus year old woman dressed in holey blue jeans and a floppy straw hat, riding a large green John Deere mower, cutting grass around the nearly two-acre property. We smiled and waved to each other and met up at the front door.

Beverly, always one to be sure food was quickly on the horizon, suggested we drop our bags and hit a Thai restaurant suitable for quiet chats in the pleasant, small local town.

While getting to know each other at lunch, Mary and I shared our dream of starting an online company that designed and produced fashion accessories based on past designs, such as hand-warmer muffs, flowing capes, and—my particular favorite—women's elegant gloves. We secretly hoped Ms. Hafemeister, whose business was recreating historic draperies for museums and private homeowners nationwide, would show interest in our project.

While chatting over a good meal, I noticed that Mary was quiet and a bit removed from the conversation. I asked her what was wrong and she admitted, "I'm feeling a little melancholy. I'm missing my mom."

I was quite surprised, after having just driven in the car with Mary for the last four hours, that she never mentioned her feelings during the drive. Equally surprising was the use of the old fashioned word *melancholy*; certainly not how Mary usually spoke. To bring Beverly up to speed, Mary went on to talk about her mother's recent passing.

As lunch came to a close, we headed back to Beverly's house. As soon as we entered the house, Mary and I both immediately felt a lot of ghost energy. Typically, I do not become aware of ghosts simply by walking into a home. Rather, I have to shift into my psychic level and scan the house to see if I find any unusual energy areas.

Immediately, Mary and I had different reactions to all this ghost energy. I started to feel a dull headache pressure build. Mary said, "I smell smoke." Mary sat down and seemed to be pulled to a male cigarette smoking energy, which was again out of character for her, because she's usually very repelled by smoke.

I sat down in the living room chair and dropped my head to focus on what was attached to my headache. When I looked up, I found not only a living room full of ghosts looking back at me, but was startled to hear loud laughter coming from a ghost party in the dining room. I reluctantly informed Beverly of all this ghost energy. I quickly stated that it was not heavy or dark, but that both rooms had plenty of occupants.

I told her the information I was obtaining from the party group. "Beverly, your unseen dining room party guests from the 1950s or 1960s appear to have come with the house and land when your uncle bought this property in 1966. They are relatives of the previous owners." I think this news flash amazed and surprised Beverly because she didn't say a thing.

Then I moved my attention back to the living room to get a handle on the group of ghosts sitting around. I sensed that these were Beverly's family members. Mary then asked Beverly if she could go upstairs. The smoking man she first sensed had been talking to her and he wanted her to see something in the upstairs hallway.

I was a bit annoyed by this request. I put myself into Beverly's shoes: an elderly woman with two strangers who had just come into her home and immediately inform her the house is full of ghosts! Now one woman wants to go into the owner's private quarters to "look for something." Sounds like a con game going on! I didn't want Beverly to have those thoughts. I tried to discourage Mary from heading up the steps, but Mary rebuffed me and said she was being instructed to do so by this ghost. Beverly said it was okay.

Mary went up.

On her return downstairs to the living room, Mary relayed what she had seen and heard. The wall at the top of the stairs displayed framed photographs of Beverly's family line. Mary said that as she wondered which of the many photos on the wall the ghost meant her to see, the man said in Mary's ear, "No, not that picture. My picture is above it to the right." It was a studio portrait of a jovial young guy lighting a cigarette. It was Beverly's uncle Arthur with his 1930s scribbled message, "When you're feeling kinda sad and blue, squint at this, and you'll laugh too. (signed) Art." Apparently, it was Uncle Art's way of cheering up Mary and telling us that he had followed us to the restaurant for lunch and knew of Mary's melancholy.

I was still a bit annoyed at Mary's boldness, and shot a dirty look at her. Then all of a sudden I was shocked when I felt the ghost of Uncle Art hit me in the chest with energy, not to hurt me, but to make clear he was being protective of Mary. I got my hackles up and told this Uncle Art, "Back off, Mister."

Feeling all the initial animosity from Uncle Art was another situation to which I wasn't accustomed, and to be honest, he was the only ghost frustrated enough to hit me with his powerful energy. This was particularly tough to take when my motive was simply to help ease discomfort for him and Beverly.

Mary went to sit in the corner chair. She appeared to be enamored with this guy and seemed to be having a little heart-to-heart talk with him. I directed my attention to the miscellaneous collection of ghosts cluttering up the living room, who were giving me one wallop of a headache.

I said, "Ghost family, just so you're aware of what's happening, Beverly can't see you like I do, so I'm going to describe each of you to her to see if she can identify you. If you give me your names, that would be brilliant. However, names require me to use my left brain and my ability to *see* you is the work of my right brain. Switching back and forth is hard. It doesn't always work, but I'll try. I'll describe what you look like to help Bev identify you. If you want to share any additional information with me at the time, feel free."

First, I described a large man sitting in the recliner. He wore a black suit with a bright white shirt, black tie, and white socks with black shoes. He had the feel of Alfred Hitchcock, not so much visually, but the same sort of calm and reserved demeanor. Unlike Hitchcock, he seemed very approachable, a very comfortable-in-his-skin type of personality.

Beverly said, "That has to be Ferdinand, my great-grandfather on my dad's side. Tranquility, inner peace, and solid demeanor were traits I recognized in my dad and in many of his family. Also, I remember a picture of Ferdinand dressed in that outfit sitting next to my great-grandmother. He died before I was born."

Standing to the right of Ferdinand was a man who identified himself as Reinhold. I described him as a bit well-to-do, because of the sporty clothes he was wearing: a cream shirt and tan knickerbockers that ended just below the knee, complete with long, cream-colored socks and darker tan shoes.

He had a patterned vest or scarf. Youthful, lean, and maybe in his early 30s, he appeared to be a nice guy. Beverly was unable to place him.

Sitting on the other side of Ferdinand was a young, beautiful woman who readily stated her name as Babette. She wore a vibrant blue flapper dress from the 1920s, but it wasn't flamboyant with sparkles and fringe as one sees in movies. She seemed quite taken by great-grandfather Ferdinand. Accompanying her was another flapper-type girl who refused to interact with me. Again, Beverly was not able to identify them.

I turned to check out the front corner of the room. Two older women sitting in facing chairs were gossiping. They weren't looking at me or answering any of my questions, but they were making snarky comments about everyone in the room. One of them was a plump woman wearing a Victorian dress and the most delicious large-brimmed purple hat topped with a large feather. Her dark hair was tied up into the hat. The lady was in deep conversation with another woman whose appearance paled in comparison, dressed in a very pale pink dress with lots of ruffles. She and the other woman were so engaged in whispered gossip that I only got their names, Helga for the woman in purple, Anna in delicate pink.

Beverly said, "Well, on my mother's side of the family, there was a favorite peacemaking great-aunt, Anna, but I'm not sure about a Helga … but excessive gossip was taken to an art form in that extended family!"

I got a chill and felt someone else. "Someone in attendance is too fearful to show a body form. She is hiding over the shoulder of Anna, right below that beautiful painting." The woman whispered to me to get up and go look closer at the painting, so I did.

The invisible woman just said, "That is my favorite painting. The warm campfire at a cool moonlit lake reflects my contrasting moods. It was painted by the same artist as my other picture Beverly has upstairs."

With that exposed, Beverly was able to identify the invisible woman as her great-aunt Louise, Ferdinand's daughter. "It's true. That was Aunt Louise's painting. There is a second picture upstairs, a wonderful, reverse pastel still life."

I then peeked into the dining room. As I started to describe those people, Helga blurted out in an uppity, dismissive tone, "They don't belong to us." I immediately knew that to be true, for the group appeared completely oblivious of the living room family.

The feeling in the dining room was electric! The hostess was dressed in a 50s skirt flared out with layers of crinoline petticoats covered by an apron, and had her hair pinned up. She carried a tray with food and drink to the men and women in attendance. The boisterous group of card players were having spirited fun. (Pun intended!)

I tried to talk with them, but they were too involved in their partying to answer.

Art now joined us in physical form in the living room and was sending out antagonistic vibes to me. I confronted him, "Uncle Art, why are you being so negative to me?" He said, "I don't know who you are and why you're here with Beverly." I told him of the invitation to stay the weekend and attend a function. He said, "I don't like it."

I told the room there had been times when I confronted a difficult ghost, but now Art headed my list of tough cases. Even if he was acting from protectiveness toward Beverly, that kind of energy was not a good environment for her.

"Art, I know you're her uncle, you're concerned about her, and I'm aware this was your home, bequeathed to Beverly. Also, I know through the stories Bev has shared, you were an artist, a furniture maker, and an interior designer who put your heart and soul into this place. But continuing to stay in this home is not good for Beverly. None of you family relatives are helping Beverly. Really, you're all hurting her by sucking on her energy. You need to understand all ghosts derive their energy from living humans. Once you have crossed out of the ghost existence, visiting Beverly or anyone else will not drain their human energy."

"That's not true! I don't believe you! I knew I didn't trust you!" yelled Arthur.

Art turned to his ally Mary. "Can you ask Beverly if it's true that I'm draining her? I don't believe that woman!"

Mary was a bit hesitant but said, "Beverly, can you hear your uncle?" Beverly sheepishly responded, "No, I can't." Mary tentatively relayed exactly what Art had just uttered in her ear.

Beverly was slow to reply for fear she would offend her uncle, but she eventually responded, saying, "I hesitate to say, but my enthusiasm and energy for things has been fading. Sometimes I wonder how long I could stay in this house. I had no idea my house was full of ghosts, or that their presence was sapping my strength. I'd been blaming my medicine."

Art announced, "I'm going to walk around the property and have a smoke."

I told the room what had happened with Art. I felt his overly defensive negative energy had deflated. I had a hunch he might be ready to cross over.

A few moments later, Art reentered the room. He said to me in a rather abrupt way, "How do we do this?"

I informed him and the other ghosts who were paying attention, "I can't make anyone cross over who does not want to go. I've had a long, tiring day, so I'm just going to help Arthur tonight. We can schedule another crossing on Sunday after our event, so watch what happens with Art and then decide if you're ready for Sunday."

"Okay, Art, are you ready?" Art was in agreement so I started the process. "Art, I want you to be comfortable about leaving the home you love. Furthermore, I appreciate your feelings about Bev since they are all based on family responsibility and protection. Understand by leaving this ghost level, you will be able to come back as often as you like to check up on Beverly, but you will no longer drain her energy. Trust me, it's best for both Beverly and you. The same message goes for the rest of the family in attendance."

"Now, I know you're the brother of Beverly's mom Eleanor, so I'm asking your sister to come and help you cross over."

I almost jumped out of my skin when Eleanor popped in right behind my chair and put her hands on my shoulders.

"Oh! There you are Eleanor. You startled me! Art, your sister is here. I realize none of you ghosts can see Eleanor, but just know she's here standing behind me. Uncle Art, I'm not sure why my guide Timingo is telling me this, but can you come sit on the floor in front of me?"

He did as requested, then Timingo reminded me about a past event where I connected two souls, one ghost and one crossed-over spirit, by using my human hand.

I gave instructions. "I'm going to put my hand out toward Arthur. Eleanor, I'd like you to put your hand *in* my arm and move it *through* into my hand. Next, Art, you touch your fingers to mine and you will see your sister."

Seconds later, both Mary and I broke out in spontaneous roaring laughter! Those in the room had no idea what had just happened, but excited energy bounced around the room. I said, "Beverly, your mother is so funny! She just did a dramatic flourish and slid an elegantly gloved hand into my hand!"

A huge look of surprise washed across Beverly's face. She said, "She must have been with us at the restaurant! That quirky sense of humor is exactly what Mother would do!"

I said to Art, who was still sitting on the floor, "Okay. Eleanor did her part, now you touch my fingers, Art." As Arthur reached up to touch my hand, the room appeared to get lighter. All the ghosts and people in the room let out an audible "Aha!" because Eleanor came into form. All saw her, except Beverly, who could not see her mom.

Eleanor coaxed, "Come on, Little Fella. We've been waiting for you!" Art broke down in tears, and *poof* they were gone.

A few seconds later I heard Art say, "Thank you," to which I replied, "You're welcome." I then informed all present that hearing his thanks meant a lot to me. Arthur was a tough spirit to cross due to his intense need to make the right decision for another, his niece Beverly. Art had been in great conflict. I sensed that to trust a stranger was a real leap of faith for him. I was exhausted, but felt brightened by his gratitude.

Beverly said she wanted to give some follow-up information on the afternoon's events. "Probably Art's trust issues with strangers sprang from being stranded in Hollywood with a friend," Bev said. "They were both swindled of their meager funds and struggled under harsh conditions to get back home to Ohio during the Great Depression."

"My mother, as Art's only sibling, was five years his senior, and as an adult, she was many inches shorter than her little brother. Calling him "Little Fella" was a long-standing family joke and probably additional proof to Art that he was seeing his sister. Hearing her teasing message probably triggered familiar feelings of safety and security that he'd been deprived of while being an earthbound ghost for the last 26 or so Earth years."

"I didn't actually see the interaction between Mother and Uncle Art," Bev added, "but I was greatly touched and glad that Mother was there for him. I want to thank you, Kym, for helping Uncle Art and, inadvertently, me. I hope the remaining family will allow you to help them on Sunday so their journey can continue."

"Well thank you, Beverly" I replied. "And to all the other family and dining room people, I promise to set up a crossing on Sunday, so don't worry. See you all then."

Beverly's Personal Journey:

With great anticipation, I looked forward to meeting Kym and her friend Mary, but I was nervous to have two such sensitive women enter my home. I enjoyed living here, but hadn't a clue as to who or what they might discover. Their initial words were comforting as they announced they felt no particular bad vibes. Gradually, they began to pick up more information about the house and my unseen, long term family residents. I didn't know what to make of it. Furthermore, I was really floored to realize Uncle Art was very much a part of the household. It had never occurred to me he might be a ghost. When the question of whether or not the ghostly presences in the household were draining me of vitality, I had to sit down and give this serious thought. Yes, actually moving here had seemed to sap me of strength decades ago.

Now, that's a delicate problem to tell the man who generously gave me the property that he was also the source of my sluggish responses. I can't imagine what he was thinking when he went for a smoke and a stroll around the property. Whatever it was, his thoughts were a brave leap into the future. The description of the crossing (remember I could see nothing) was a delight and typical of this sibling relationship between the two people I hold dear to my heart. What a treasure!

Since this is the only chapter written without the benefit of an audio record, Kym and I relived the afternoon's events in our minds to capture the details. One sticky point was the question of where my mother was during lunchtime.

I insisted she must have been with us at lunch to know about Kym's love of elegant gloves. Otherwise, why would she have made a big joke of sweepingly flaunting her gloved hand at Uncle Art's crossing?

To the contrary, Kym insisted she saw Mother remain in the living room as a quiet listener of family news relayed by assorted ghostly relatives. As a crossed-over spirit she was able to see and hear them, but she was invisible to them.

Finally, Kym and I remembered back to the first reading with Hal when he told us crossed-over spirits could be in more than one place at a time. Of course! We recognized then how firmly we are ensconced in our earthly beliefs. We hadn't really absorbed all the concepts to embrace fully the knowledge of spirithood abilities. Our disagreement ended immediately; we had both been correct as to the location of Mother.

Kym's Professional Journey:

There was a lot of new information that I learned from Beverly's family. It seemed to be hidden in the nuances, so for the benefit of both myself and you the reader, I'll break down the information for us to digest it more easily.

Ghost Abilities:

- Ghosts can decide where they want to hang out. Uncle Art chose to stay in his beloved home. Beverly who was the family historian collected ancestral memorabilia including personal items of these ghost family members. The ghosts were attracted to both Beverly and their personal possessions.
- Different groups of ghosts can inhabit the same place, but not interact with each other, such as the dining room people and living room people.
- Not all ghosts around you are related to you in any way. The dining room group were not relatives of Beverly.
- Ghosts are not limited to a location they inhabit. They can travel about. Art came to the restaurant with us and listened to our conversation as did Eleanor.
- Moral compasses stay intact in ghost form. Uncle Art was protective and loyal to Beverly. His lack of trust in not believing me about his effect on Beverly's health came through clearly.

- Prejudices also stay intact. Helga was sure to point out, "They don't belong to us," in reference to the dining room people. Helga and Anna's gossipy, judgmental ways were still in full force.
- Fears stay intact as well. Aunt Louise never showed herself in body form.
- Ghosts have the ability to throw energy that can hit the living. Art's energy hit me; but note, I have never had this happen to me before, nor have I experienced it after this event. So in my professional view, this is rare.
- Ghosts are people. To get them to move on with their journey is a matter of explaining to them the details of their situation and their options. It's no great magic, just reasoning.
- Ghosts can be attracted to someone who is living and interact with them. Uncle Art and Mary's instant connection is an example.
- Ghosts can make a choice whether to show themselves in body form or not. I didn't see Art in form in the beginning, and Aunt Louise never showed herself.

Crossed Spirit Abilities:

- Spirits can travel about and follow whomever they want and listen in on private talks. At the restaurant Eleanor learned about Kym's affinity for elegant period gloves.
- The sense of humor of spirits is still intact. The dramatic flair of Eleanor wearing her long, lovely gloves was homage to my interest in this fashion accessory.

As a medium, I never know what I'm walking into in a situation. I was planning on a lovely, quiet weekend getaway and ended up dealing with unexpected ghosts. And, the ghostly experience only became more intense before the weekend was over!

Personal Growth Questions:

1. Think back to the cargo pilot dream in Chapter 7. Do you see a connection to this chapter? Is it a sample of cosmic humor with some of the joke still obscured?
2. As Kym explained to the ghosts that were telling her their names, she needed to bounce from her left brain to her right brain, and even then she might not be able to get names. What do you think about this?
3. When Kym was going to check in with the dining room ghosts, Helga yelled out, "They don't belong to us." Did you ever think ghosts would still display prejudices? What are your thoughts?

A Mega Family Reunion

April 28, 2013, Beverly's Mindset

From the quiet of the kitchen, I could hear the muffled early morning sounds from the two upstairs bedrooms which told me Kym and Mary were awake. Footsteps in and out of the bathroom announced they were in various stages of getting ready for this Sunday's event. As I rummaged around putting together the simple breakfast, my thoughts were only on the activity planned for eight o'clock am. We were to participate in crossing a group of ghosts over to the other side. Mary had assured me, as a statement of her faith, that all was planned down to the last detail on the other side. The success of the event, I was told, depended on the roles we three humans were to play.

Until yesterday, I'd never been aware of a ghost presence around my house, much less witnessed a group crossing of such people. True to form, I was tense and timidly afraid. Then suddenly, I heard for the first time today an equally weak, worried voice in my head. A lady ghost was talking to me. It was my great-aunt Louise, but I'm not sure how I knew. She'd heard a crossing was to take place shortly, but she didn't know what to do. Her family was planning to accept the invitation to travel onward. She, however, was trying to decide if she had the courage to face the unknown with them. On the other hand, if she decided to stay in my house, Aunt Louise was terrified of being alone when the rest of her ghostly family had gone. Could I please advise her?

I never felt more ill-prepared to counsel someone in my life. I had no practical knowledge. What ghostly entities would remain here? If they were anything like the spirit voices I had been confronting for the last couple of years, it would be truly unpleasant for Aunt Louise to stay here, being the fragile woman I remember. Regretfully, I had no solid understanding of what was on the other side other than what I learned yesterday from my mother's and uncle's interaction.

Surely, Aunt Louise saw I was frightened myself, so I suggested she look for answers from someone else. And yes, I was ashamed of my response of shooing her away. It was the last I heard of her until I heard a rumbling from ghosts whom I assumed were family. It appears that no one could find her, although the crossing was about to commence. My heart sank because now I felt responsible for her well-being.

After a token breakfast, the three of us women sat ourselves in a semicircle in the living room as Kym turned on the recorder to record the event. I was anxious, but I figured Kym knew what she was doing.

Beverly (B), Kym (K), and Mary (M)

K: For this ghost crossing, we each have a team. Kym and Timingo, Beverly and her guide, and Mary and Carl. From the other side are Beverly's mother, Eleanor; her newly crossed-over uncle, Arthur; and her longtime friend, Hal; and their guides.

To connect the team's energy, we need to join by touching fingertips. Girls, let's touch hands and our crossed spirit members can link up to my and Mary's free hands to complete the circle. All the spirit guides are standing behind us.

Oh! My fingers started tingling.

M: So have mine.

[*Kym was pulled out of her body and was taken up above Beverly's house. For miles she saw ghosts coming from all directions. Then, she returned to her body in the living room.*]

K: [*to the spirits and people of her team*] We're going to be here a while because the entire property just filled up with ghosts. Move your light over to the fireplace and join with mine to make it more powerful. The ghosts will see the fireplace as a lighted doorway to enter.

Beverly, you can start saying the Lord's Prayer and we'll chime in.

B: Our Father, who art in heaven hallowed be thy name ... [*everyone joins in*]

K: This morning we're asking God to come into this room to join all of his workers and all people of faith. We ask this be a holy place full of love, affection, and no judgment or fear. [*Kym saw the room light up. Suddenly the spirits in the circle, Eleanor, Arthur, and Hal, came into form so the ghosts could finally see them all.*]

It's working! They see your mom ... [*The ghosts could see the crossed-over spirits because the earthbound humans were making the connection between the levels by touching hands with them*.]

[*to reluctant ghosts*] Ghosts who are afraid or uncertain can move to the end of the line and decide later if they want to go. This is a free-will opportunity.

[*to the line of ghosts outside the house*] You folks can come in the back door and go into the light. I ask you to do it quickly because there are so many wanting to leave. I'm asking Beverly's family, who've been living in the house with her, to wait until the end. Just sit comfortably and watch this miraculous process.

Mentally, I'll open up the back door. The ghosts are filtering in. I hope you all can feel the happiness! [*Kym feels the emotion from the ghosts walking up to the light.*]

[*Beverly is crying. Her reaction to the intense wave of happiness flowing out from the crowd resulted in tears. She absorbed the emotion, but not through the regular five senses.*]

K: Why are these average people being punished by being ghosts? That question overwhelms me. They are just farmers, housewives, field workers, children. All these souls stayed for some reason… all I know is they're ready to move on.

[*to Beverly*] For any ghosts who are afraid, including your family, seeing this joy has got to bring hope! It's amazing! [*laughing*] Oh, my gosh, my body just tingles with the crossing ghosts' excitement!

M: I know, so is mine!

K: [*to Beverly*] Oh! Do you feel some large things coming into your house?

B: No, is that Rudy? [*Rudy is her deceased horse who she actually told to wait for her on the other side under the care of her deceased father.*]

K: No, not Rudy but there are other horses. Men are with their horses asking if they can take them in. I said, "Absolutely."

B: Maybe they've seen my car bumper stickers supporting humane treatment of horses?

K: Don't know. There's a range of beautiful plow horses, and sadly, some exhausted horses.

B: How nice of the owners to remember their animals, even as ghosts.

K: No, I think it's the animals who remembered their owners. The animals are in ghost form, so they must have either waited for their owners or followed them. It seems the love the animal had for their owners has kept them as ghosts. All kinds of animals are here. I see dogs. One woman has four or five dogs with her. She obviously was a huge dog lover, and they loved her too. They all waited for her to cross.

M: I see a woman baker with lattice-crust pies. She's bringing the pies with her.

K: [*looking at the backyard*] There's a lot of kibitzing and socializing going on in the line! Interesting! I saw a string of guys with big feed sacks over their shoulders walking in.

Bringing symbols of their jobs is their way of telling us who they are.

M : Smiling children with full faces and chunky legs said, “We’re going on an adventure!”

K: I felt a huge energy wave flow out of the light, rush out the door, and down the line of ghosts as an announcement: “The light is here!” The ghosts’ anticipation builds!

[*to Beverly*] Wow! The ghosts in the dining room just came out! They're standing in the doorway to see what's going on.

There's no hesitation by the people in line anymore. Usually, I get a question or two. Now they're just focused on the fireplace doorway. Beverly and Mary, in your mind's eye you can walk over and look into the light to feel it for yourself. Don’t worry, the energy won’t drag you in. I don't think it would let you enter anyway.

Peek inside. See what's on the other side.

B : To tell you the absolute truth, with closed eyes, I've not been hearing anything in my head, however, intermittently I see a glorious purple color which sometimes takes the form of an eye. As far as walking over to the fireplace, I don't see a door with the light. Concentrating and generating my personal light plus saying the Lord’s Prayer is probably enough for me now.

K : All right. Were you able to go look at the light, Mary? What did you see?

M : When I was outside the light, I was inquisitive. My guide, Carl, said I could only walk up halfway into the tunnel. As I started walking, the energy is gentle, inviting, peaceful. As the tunnel bent to the right, I wanted to run further. But they're pushing me back saying, “It's not your time. All in good time.”

K: I can never see deeply into the light. I see only people who are standing close to the opening, ready to welcome loved ones. They're shapes without details, but I can feel the light’s warmth and the tug of the energy.

M: I always see a tunnel which feels accommodating. You can walk through there alone or ten abreast without anybody stumbling over anyone else.

B: But you still see people going in?

Kym and Mary: [simultaneously] Oh, yes!

K: I see some Indians come in. Amazing how many animals are still coming in.

B: It's a farm community.

K: I don't see cows and goats. I see mostly dogs, cats, and horses. Maybe cows and sheep are not domesticated enough to make that human connection and decide to stay? I don't know.

B: Dogs, cats, and horses can develop a bond with humans by working and living together.

K: I see women in stiffly starched white dresses with hats. Their long dresses with apron overlays are not form fitting. Could be a nun's outfit. The hats they're wearing flip up, but not like Sally Field's *Flying Nun* habit. Sally's looked like a wing on both sides of her head, but these women's hats are like a 'V' with a small downward flip at the tip. Maybe it was an order in this vicinity.

Yes, they're nuns. I just heard them praying. I'm confused why so many women would stay behind after their death. Oh, my impression is they were all killed together! Men came where they were working or living. They raped them and killed them all. The nuns believed they died in shame. Now, the pain is no longer there because they dealt with the shame on the ghost level. Reverently in prayer, they're walking into the light together.

[*to a ghost in line*] Ah, no, you can't drive that in here. Leave it outside! Really, you won't need that on the other side.

[*to the group*] This guy has a Ford Model T he loves. I've let guys walk in with bicycles, but not cars!

A lot of religious people are coming in. I think these people believed if they waited, the Lord would raise them up from the dead. What they thought would happen, didn't.

The line hasn't slowed down but keeps getting longer and longer. Ghosts are coming from the road and all sides of the house. People have been waiting for a long time to cross. I don't know how that works. [*snarkily*] Does a newsletter go out announcing there's going to be a ghost crossing at Beverly's house?

B: [*smiling*] Possibly not. However, having a big turnout is not surprising. Being in a rural area there probably aren't many people like you capable of crossing people over.

K: This happened to me another time. When in Savannah, I went to a slave cemetery in a side yard between a house and a church. It was so small it wasn't marked as a cemetery on any map. With the few cemetery markers, I didn't anticipate many ghosts. When I opened the light, a large grouping of black slaves including a few white men from a higher class, came from all directions. How a pending crossing is broadcast is a mystery to me. The announcement system worked well, because I was quickly overwhelmed by the crowd, but kept the light open as long as I could. Obviously, the number of ghosts to be crossed over has nothing to do with cemetery capacity.

Lots of conversation is going on in this house now. Before there was a happy card party going on in the dining room with plenty of laughter and drinking. Now there is a murmur. Ghosts in the dining room are talking about the line and saying, "Can all those people be wrong?"

A little boy broke through the line and ran into the light. Wow! He went in all by himself!

[*to Beverly*] Ferdinand, your great-granddad, just walked up to your mom and asked her, "Can I hold your hand and join the circle?" She said, "No, not yet. You have to cross first." He looked disappointed, but humbly said, "Oh, pardon me." He sat back down.

Oh, I didn't know that was a requirement: I guess his ghost energy is not compatible with what we're doing.

M: A band of angels is herding all the people outside to make sure they all get into the house.

K: I see two ghosts struggling with their mutual headstone out in the yard. [*to the two girls holding the headstone*] Hey, you don't need that headstone. The girls asked, "How will they know who we are?"

[*to the girls*] They will. Don't worry, you can go in like you are. You'll keep your sense of your body. They'll know who you are. Angels, help these two girls put down their headstone and bring them to the front of the line.

These two sisters, Amelia & Rosanne Wilcox, died together of the fever.

[*to the girls*] You will not be forgotten. You will not die.

The sisters just asked, "Will we turn to dust?"

[*to the girls*] No, people don't disintegrate when they enter the light.

Knowing they are not going to turn to dust, the girls are excited now.

[*to the girls*] Go on in together. Aw, they're holding hands.

B: Since I can't see anything, did you say that Ferdinand could see my mother?

K: Yes. Remember, once we all connected by touching hands, ghosts could see the crossed-over spirits.

B : Of course. He would have known Mother through his daughter Louise. Did I miss that, did Ferdinand cross yet?

K: No, he sat back down to cross with your family members. He just wanted to have this experience of holding energy for crossing ghosts. I don't think Ferdinand has any quandaries about crossing, but I've yet to see his daughter Louise. Yesterday, I felt her talk to me about her favorite painting but never physically saw her.

There's a whole group of businessmen here, not sure what they want to do. A spokesman stepped forward to say they are men who owned small shops which formed an early town. I asked him if he meant Cincinnati. He said no.

[*talking to the group*] As much as I hate to rush you ghosts along, we've got to get moving. We're already moving at a good pace, but even at this rate we'll be here all night. Angels, if you could help move them even faster, I'd appreciate it.

I'm seeing more fashionably dressed women in high style now. Many people are from Kentucky. They showed me horse racing and gambling.

B: It might be the Kentucky Derby, which was a big, high society event with a national presence.

K: These are a couple of northern women, not southerners.

[*to the ladies*] Did you die in Kentucky? One woman is saying, "No, we didn't die at the Kentucky Derby, but it was one of our favorite social events." She's from Maine or New England area. Coming to Kentucky was a highlight in her life. Therefore, she dresses for the Derby. I now see pioneers driving their horse-drawn Conestoga wagons.

In Savannah, I saw ghost groups sorted into categories: All the yellow fever victims were together, next came a large section of wealthy Victorian men and women, followed by the prostitutes, barkeepers, and madams. The final group was from the high-end cruise ships. Unfortunately, I didn't get much detailed information crossing over such a large number. This crossing isn't like Savannah. It's a hodgepodge of eras, classes, and lifestyles.

B: A more democratic mixture here.

K: Timingo just told me to talk to the house folks.

Dining room people, can all of you come into the living room? Have you decided to go? [*they didn't come into the living room*] If you're uncertain, go poke your head in the light and you'll see there's a party over there, too.

K: A young guy from the dining room is curious and poked his head out. He's the one having so much fun. For some reason, he looks and speaks differently to me. He feels like a privileged guy with higher education. Very campy, bouncy, happy. Might be a 1920s college student. He walked over to the light.

[*to the young guy*] You see, there's a party in there, too. Everyone's fine. How about joining them?

He said, "All-righty," then ran over to the door and said to the group, "Get up!" He turned his back to them and put his hands on his hips, then mimicking conga line music, he sang, "da-da da-da da- dah." [*laughing*] They jumped up, followed suit all linking into his conga line. The hostess, still wearing her little apron and her hair all pinned up, joins the conga line last, like a good hostess! "da-da da-da da- dah." I actually heard the music! "da-da da-da da- dah." They serpentined around the spirits in our circle and danced into the light. They are the most creative ghosts I've ever crossed!

B: Fabulous!

K: I'm trying to end this crossing, but ghosts are still coming in from the back door.

[*to Beverly's family in the living room*] All right, family ... Oh, here come the two girls from upstairs running down. Mary and Beverly, I didn't tell you this, but when I was getting ready for the A.R.E event yesterday, I met these two girls in the upstairs bedroom. We were all vying for the same dressing mirror. They're now ready to go too!

Oh, good! The backyard line is coming to an end.

Ferdinand is asking his family if they're ready. He's standing, implying he wants to go with the other people. Ferdinand went over to Helga and Anna, the older women holding hands, and said, "Ladies." He put out his elbows for them both to insert their arms to be securely linked.

As they passed, Helga and Anna said, "Beverly, you never quite gave us the gossip we would have liked, but we enjoyed your company. You had stories." Ferdinand led them into the light, but did not enter himself.

[*to Beverly*] I guess when you thought about things or talked out loud, they heard you. It was gossip to them. Also, you were feeding them stories about your family keepsakes, when you were talking to the plumber or mailman. They would have liked more!

B: The old aunts didn't necessarily know each other in life, but they sure know each other in death!

K: Reinhold just came over to escort the two young flapper girls. One of them, Babette, says, "You loved us, therefore, it was always a party here with all the love." Nice message for you, Bev. Now they all walked into the light.

[*calling out*] Aunt Louise, are you ready? Beverly, did you hear her? What did she say to you?

B: [*surprised*] I'm hearing her say, "I want to go, but I'm afraid."

K: Okay, Ferdinand, can you take your daughter's hand?

B: Louise wants to take her favorite picture with her.

K: Take it with you, at least the energy part of it. The physical part will stay here.

B: Louise is saying, "I can't lift it. Will somebody help me?"

K: All right. Ferdinand, can you help Louise take the spirit of her favorite picture with her? Ferdinand said, "I'd be happy to."

[*to Louise*] Do you want to lean on your father?

Ferdinand said, "It's been an honor to be here. You're a wonderful hostess, Beverly." They both walked into the light with the picture tucked under Ferdinand's arm.

B: From the light, Louise says, "I'm happy now and I thank you. Girl, you've done good!"

K: That's exactly what I heard, too! [*laughing*]

B: I couldn't have done it without all of you in the circle.

K: No, your family is saying these sentiments are addressed to you, not to the group. They so appreciate your help, Beverly.

Who else wants to go? Who's standing behind us and not letting me see you? Who else is here?

M: There's a little boy behind me.

B: [*hearing a little boy*] He's afraid to go.

K: [*to the room*] Who will take this little boy?

B: The boy says, "I don't know if I'll find my mother there."

M: I'll take him halfway if someone will meet me.

K: The two girls from upstairs are still by the fireplace and said they'll take him. One of the girls said to the little boy, "Come on, we'll find your mom." Oh! Did you hear that?

M: No, but I just got chilled all over.

K: He yelled "Mommy!" [*laughing*] He didn't even get in the door and Mommy was waiting. That was wild! She found him! And he saw her right away!

B: I should have spoken earlier. The little boy told me, "She died a long time ago." He was concerned about finding his mother.

K: [*to the people in the room who are not allowing themselves to be seen*] See, ladies and gentlemen behind me? [*singing*] Come out. Come out, wherever you are. If the little boy could do it … Come on, he found his mommy, and he wasn't even in the door! Come on out.

I see an average-sized woman with a unique hat that obscures much of her face. She's in a tightly closed winter coat and trying to hide from me. The man behind her has a chiseled face, nice jawline, and dark gray hair poking out from under his hat. He's carrying an umbrella and wearing a gray coat, gloves, and leather business shoes. His collar is pulled up, like they've been out in the Chicago winter.

B: Maybe she's wearing a cloche hat which was a popular close-fitting millinery style in the 1920s.

K: When I first saw her, I felt shame. She's keeping her head down. I think she's trying to rush into the light without having to talk to me.

[*to the woman*] Slow down, dear. Does Beverly know you?

[*to Bev*] Okay, I got that she's related to you, but she was on the fringe of the family. I feel she and the man lived in Chicago. Do you know anyone who lived in Chicago?

B: Aunt Carrie? She lived in Chicago. Mother called her Aunt Carrie, but she wasn't really an aunt. She was Mother's and Grandmother's friend.

K: I don't know why she feels embarrassed. She wants to go quickly for some reason.

M: My spirit guide, Carl, is telling me Eleanor's family talked badly about her. She didn't defend herself, she just shied away.

B: Mother was the only one who stayed in touch with her. I remember many times as a kid stopping in Chicago for a short visit on the way to Milwaukee. And yes, the Cincinnati bunch in those days had an active, gossipy grapevine!

K: It's why she's humiliated. Gossip is cruel. She was such a sweet soul. Idle talk really damaged her. She internalized the disapproval of others, which caused her to shame herself. Therefore, Aunt Carrie described herself as being on the fringe of the family.

B: Can she see Mother now?

K: She's not even looking. [*to Carrie*] Do you see Eleanor?

B: Does Carrie know where Mother is located in the room? Kym, maybe you can point to Mother so she can see her.

K: [*to Carrie while pointing to Eleanor*] Yes, she's right over there. Oh, she won't even look up, she's so mortified! That hat is perfect for her, it covers her face.

[*to Eleanor*] Can you go say something to this poor girl? She just wants to run in. Don't let …

Your mother just split! I saw an energy of Eleanor just pull out of her body, yet another part is still in the circle holding my hand. She divided out another full impression of herself that moved quickly into the light! Eleanor went to the light and yet she's still sitting here holding my hand! How is that possible?

Eleanor is standing in the doorway of the light. She put her hand out. Now, Carrie saw her extended hand, grabbed it, and started crying. She and the man briskly walked in.

Oh, that poor soul has been tortured. I'm chilled all over. How sad! See what gossip and mean spiritedness can do to a tender soul? Now there's just great happiness. Poof! They're gone.

B: "Great happiness here" is what I was hearing from the light.

K: Okay, you hiding living room ghosts, I feel you but I'm still unable to see you. Anybody else want to go? [*pleading*] Come on. This is your time, the other line is done. They've all gone into the light. Anybody else ready to go? No?

Okay. So, for all those who did not want to cross at this junction, it's fine. We'll be able to help you in the future when you are ready. Don't worry, we will help you, but until then you have to be respectful of Beverly and her energy. You can't deplete it. So you all have to move out of the house. Stay off the property, too. Wait out there until our return.

Trust me, Beverly, you'll feel much better. You have fewer ghosts around you now, so they won't be so draining on your energy.

First, I want to thank everybody for helping us. Thanks to the angels for coming in and corralling everybody, and for Mom, Uncle Art, Hal, our guides. Let's do a complete house clearing to get all the ghost energy out.

[*The crossing and clearing were over. Kym and everyone disbanded. The following conversation between Mary and Beverly was accidentally recorded.*]

M: Beverly, how are you doing?

B: Okay, thank you, but somebody's angry at me. He's saying,"You haven't heard the last of me."

M: Allow whatever ghosts that stayed behind to know they must deal with it themselves since they didn't take the opportunity to leave. You know you did what was right. Sending souls back to God is the right thing. And that's all we did. We gave them an opportunity. If they didn't take it, it's on them.

B: The crossing was very gentle and I thank you. I don't know whether this is just my fear talking. Ironic. Here I was sitting in the exact same spot, repeating the Lord's Prayer, just as I was before going into the hospital in 2010. Perhaps I was crossing people at that time and didn't know it. I didn't think of the irony until today's crossing. I'm realizing things I once perceived as bad were really good and helping me.

But I'm hearing that man again, "You'll be sorry," in my head, even after the house was cleared out of ghosts. Something is not adding up.

Beverly's Personal Journey:

This crossing proved to be a revelation to me on several fronts, especially in relation to my genealogical pursuits. In chapter 7 you read the dream where my witty spirit guide depicted me as a cargo pilot unknowingly traveling with a family camping out in the plane's tail section. I can now see that the laugh was on me. Was this dream actually a prophetic dream, and referring to the family of ghosts who had actually been camping out in my home for years? If so, my miscellaneous invisible family ghosts were certainly in on my journey, as my dream foretold!

Of primary fascination in this crossing was my great-grandfather Ferdinand. He was my mystery patriarch for whom I have been searching for decades. A middle-aged family man with his second wife, they came to Wisconsin in 1881 from old Pommern, a region in what was then Germany on the shores of the Baltic Sea. I was curious to know about his first wife and village life as a youth in the early 19th century. After much searching on my part, his prior life experiences have yet to be discovered.

Now knowing that same ghostly great-grandfather liked sitting in the living room recliner upon which I flopped daily to watch television, I found it uproariously funny to know the man I wanted to meet and interview was in my living room all the time! Probably I've been sitting on his lap every day without knowing it.

Finally consciously meeting Ferdinand at the mass crossing, I was impressed with his focus on this crossing event and his desire to be of service in the activity. His gentlemanly escorting of the ladies, Helga and Anna, to the light and his courtly manners towards his daughter Louise with her fear of the future without her favorite picture helped me appreciate what a kindly soul he was. These traits were much like his grandson, my dad. I wondered what life events had shaped him.

One event that was sure to have changed Ferdinand was a chilling mystery I stumbled upon decades ago. While investigating my family history, I found one isolated piece of evidence written without details in our family's German Bible, just the name Emil Otto Hafemeister. Who was this man? How did he fit onto the family genealogical tree? No other accounts of who this person was were located until I saw this name again on the internment register of the huge cemetery where Ferdinand happened to work late in life. Was that just a coincidence? I had even gone so far as to drive past the single plot, viewed the sturdy stone marker, and pondered if this man could be related to my family line in some way?

I couldn't drop it. Was this the same Emil in our family Bible? Searching further, I was pleased to find my hunch was right. Emil was my blood relative. However, I was shocked and distressed to read the old daily newspaper accounts and the actual sworn court testimony transcriptions of an official inquiry describing the mysterious disappearance of Emil, who was Ferdinand's son and Louise's brother, the evening before his wedding. The court testimony tracked two frantic searches for Emil by the family when he had not returned home by the wee hours of his wedding day. No trace of him was found after he had left his favorite bar in his usual congenial mood that evening.

Just hours later, waiting at the church door, the loving bride-to-be, Ella, received crushing news that Emil was missing. One can only imagine the gamut of thoughts and emotions that raced through her mind as the guests arrived for the ceremony. Fiancée, family, friends—all had to endure day after day the uncertainty of the unknown concerning the whereabouts of Emil. A full week later came the overwhelmingly shocking news. Emil's body was fished out of the river. He had been shot with one deadly bullet that fateful night. What a crushing blow I felt as I read the literature. To live the actual experience must have been heart wrenching!

Update: Over a hundred years later, as Kym and I sat doing the final edit before publication on the paragraph above, Kym was inundated with relentless waves of chills. What was the reason? Much to our amazement it was to herald the arrival of the gregarious Emil himself, who was totally thrilled to be remembered. He was saddened, knowing he had virtually been forgotten on Earth except in that single Bible entry, a dusty court record, flimsy microfilmed newspapers, and a tombstone.

In our brief introductory encounter, Kym described his energy as effervescent and vivacious. It fit perfectly for this cheerful, charming young man. His energy confirmed for her that at the time of his death he was still the basically happy guy who was eagerly looking forward to his marriage to Ella back in 1903. While we conversed with Emil, he spoke tenderly about the pain he caused his fiancée.

Unknown to Ella and others, dice had become his secret addiction. Unfortunately, a scuffle over the gambling debt he had accumulated occurred the night before his wedding and ended with him being accidentally shot. About his murder he said, "I'm ashamed to say, *my luck* ran out," which answers my curiosity of his death and also says a lot about his sense of humor.

Emil said the fellow who sent out the thugs to rough him up a little for the dice wager money he owed, which lead to his unfortunate demise, had himself been killed two years later. Apparently now without any residual dislike for the man, as crossed-over spirits they actually hang out with each other on the other side.

With relief and gratitude, he spoke of no longer being engulfed by addictions in his life. To update us further, he has not reincarnated since the Emil life and is undecided as to what his next move will be. However, Emil said he keeps in touch with his immediate family members wherever they are. In fact, he first heard of us and our book work through his father once Ferdinand arrived on the other side after his stint as an observant ghost. Emil asked to keep in touch with us, for he'd like to be a part of this book process.

Emil also let us in on some specific information about new work his father Ferdinand has undertaken. It's too much of a brain twister for this book, so we'll have to wait until a later book when Kym and I unscramble it. Consequently, we expect this isn't the last you'll hear from this father and son duo in our series.

I'm happy to know Emil wants to keep in touch, because, once discovered all those years ago, I've always felt a special fondness for him, never guessing I would actually meet him in a spontaneous session. Also, what a wonderful opportunity for us to learn from another perspective, another viewpoint on life after life on the other side of what is quickly becoming a less invisible structure to Kym and me.

I think of the conversations I already missed out on with my family because I didn't know they were living with me in ghost form. Perhaps I could have heard them if I had been willing and brave. Now, as I mourn the loss of a past opportunity, Emil just opened wide another communication door!

Kym's Professional Journey:

I'd like to address a few unique points about this crossing session. First, this was the first time I did such a formal set up with prayers and hand holding, let alone bringing in crossed spirits into the process. All of this was directed to me by Timingo. I also had no idea that asking Beverly to say the Lord's Prayer would be a powerful reminder of her previous terrifying experience when she was urged by feverish voices compelling her to say this prayer over and over again. She did not realize the repeated request for her prayers was the petition of those folks who were helping to protect her. I was happy she got a new view of this event's purpose. Perhaps with this new understanding, she might surmise that she had also been crossing over souls during that time.

In this mass crossing we are given more information about the abilities of ghosts:

- Ghosts have many of the same hang-ups as live humans do. The young sisters with their headstone were asking, "Will they know us?"
- Ghosts identify who they are by the job they had, such as the men carrying feed bags and the baker with her pies.
- Ghosts can't see crossed spirits unless the living help connect them by touching.
- Ghosts feel excitement about leaving their ghostly existence.
- Ghosts hold on to great life memories, such as the woman attending the Kentucky Derby.
- Ghosts keep religious beliefs, such as the girls thinking they might turn to dust once they walked into the light.

- Judging from the number of animals in attendance in the crossing, it seems ghosts keep their love and connection to animals.

Ghosts carry deep shame: such as the nuns, Aunt Carrie, and the entire section that chose not to leave at this crossing.

We also learned something ghosts can't do: ghosts can't be involved in the crossing of other ghosts. When Eleanor declined Ferdinand's interest in helping with the crossing, it was because ghost energy is too dense before they cross over themselves.

As for the interaction with Emil, I was thrilled to hear his story and all the fascinating facts he told us about how he died. I'm glad that Beverly now has that missing piece to her family history. I hope to interview him in future books. He was such a lovely energy to channel.

My experience with Beverly has been a constant surprise and has consisted of many firsts for me personally. In the next chapter my new training continues. Never has Timingo asked me outside of a scheduled session to contact a client, unless it was an emergency. Timingo apparently felt Beverly needed a validation letter. I was glad to assist in his reaching out in the next chapter.

Personal Growth Questions:

1. Aunt Carrie was a ghost who carried great shame as a result of vicious gossip about her. Think about how gossip has touched you or someone close to you. Write out your thoughts on gossip.
2. At the end of the crossing, Mary and Bev were talking and Bev shared a new viewpoint. "I'm realizing things I once perceived as bad, were really good and helping me." What do you think about this statement? Have you found yourself having the same realization in your life?
3. What were your thoughts and feelings about the ghosts who arrived? Were you surprised at the variety of distinctive personalities they represented? The variety of eras? The assortment of religious beliefs expressed? Their patience?

Pep Talk from the Other Side

May 16, 2013, Kym's Mindset

This morning Timingo appeared and asked a favor of me. Would I transcribe a letter to Beverly from him and mail it to her? I was surprised for he had never made such a request before. Below is a copy of his letter.

Letter to Beverly Hafemeister from Timingo:

Beverly, the experience you had with Kym and Mary was a gift to you from all of us on the other side. The girls would not see themselves that way, as gifts, but their humility is just that—theirs! We see them, and you as well, as great gifts to our cause of helping all trapped souls on the Earth plane and beyond.

Your work has been so much more than you have been aware. We are grateful you have found the courage to persevere through your human issues of fear and of your worry about being "crazy." The problem is you were not aware we were by your side; you have never been alone on this journey. Your fear blocked you in a very clear way from holding our hands.

That is the past, we are happy to say. We have seen and felt the new embrace of what you are called to do. The fear wall you had up against us has been removed. We see you in all your brilliance.

We want to thank you for being such an amazing trooper. Know that we are always just a question or thought away. You have the girls, Kym and Mary, to call on in the earth plane. You are not crazy nor have you ever been. Hold on to that!

We are also sorry you questioned that in the past. We really did not send you back unprepared. You were versed in your work on the Earth plane, even if it doesn't appear that way to you. I promise you were! In the course of your work's purpose for us on this side, you had some tidbits of experience you wanted to test. Working through self-doubt was one of them. So, in the midst of your work for us, it allowed you to test that very issue. You are a strong and experienced soul, but you forgot that just to have this self-doubt experience. Please doubt it no more! Know you are a trooper; it will keep you steadfast on your mission.

Also, know that we are all very proud of you and the girls. We have so many more happy souls here because of all the wonderful work you did together as a group.

Oh, your mother wants to chime in …

Bevy, you did me and your father proud for your courage and strength that you have always shown, but it was never more apparent than when you were struggling in the hospital. We never left your side. We encouraged you, we held you in your darkest moments, we kissed the top of your head until it was raw. We loved you and still do.

I'm so grateful to you for helping our family (who lived in your living room) to move on in their soul journey. They are a very happy bunch now and so happy to be free of the restraints of the Earth experience. They have already been back to check in on you, so don't feel they have gone on to greener pastures without you. You are with all of us all the time! Just talk with us and we will be there, just like always, but now you are not so afraid of "going crazy." That issue has passed. Just turn to us and to your new friends for support.

I love you, baby, and I'll be front and center when you come home again.

Timingo here again. Beverly, so many want to come into this note, but I know Kym needs to get on with some of her work. Therefore, I told them they can talk to you directly if they need to. Don't be surprised if you hear them! They seem to be a chatty bunch!

Take care Beverly, and know you are all powerful and have no need to have fear. You are a warrior.

Kindest regards,

Timingo

Note From Kym:

Wow, Beverly! Timingo has never written someone a note through me before! I have known for a few weeks that he wanted to talk with you, but I got kind of busy with stuff in my own life. However, this morning, he made it clear that this was the day. I'm not concerned, I know this note will find you when it was meant to be received by you.

Enclosed is a CD of the audio of the event. I have it on my list to transcribe, but it might be quite a while before I get to it. I am doing a lot of client work with past lives which also requires transcription, so I'm bogged down. Plus, I'm really trying to get back to writing my books. If you are good at transcribing your session, and if you have time to make a hard copy, please send me a copy.

Take care, sweet Beverly. Mary and I plan on coming out to see you once more this summer. No agenda, just visiting. But then again, we never know what happens when three such powerful chicks get together. All I know is that it's never boring!

Love you lots,

Kym

Email Reply from Beverly:

Hi Kym,

I think you've got a couple of splendid ideas many people would be fascinated to hear.

You've got a lot of good information tucked away in your brain, it's time to share it. Write! I encourage you to expose what you are learning with those who are willing to listen. Many will listen and benefit; many will not, because it's not time for them to receive new thoughts.

The more practical response to your messages to me is - sure I can make a transcription for you. I'm waiting for some drapery trim to arrive for a job I'm doing, so I can't do any sewing right now. Therefore, I've got a couple free days to transcribe the crossing CD and type up a copy for you. It would be fun to transcribe and to notice details of what took place that morning.

In closing, I want to thank Timingo and you both for the fabulous letter. I'm honored and, as usual, speechless. When he tells me that my work has been so much more than I have been aware, it really resonates with me. If anyone walks blindly through life, it's certainly me! If there is praise and accolades, the reason for it puzzles me, but I'm happy the results are beneficial. Details and descriptions will come one day.

If you'll forgive me, I'll trot out my quirky sense of humor one more time when I heehaw at the thought of my parents kissing the top of my head until it was raw. Here, all the time I was thinking it was alopecia or the chants. Really, it was too many kisses had fatigued my follicles! My family appreciates my humor so I can imagine Mother is chuckling brightly. Dad gives his canny smile.

Well Kym, one weird joke is probably enough, so I bid you adieu. Keep in touch and keep up the good work!

Beverly

Kym's Professional Journey:

Dear Reader, the purpose of including this chapter with the letter from Timingo to Beverly was to let you see how my simple complaint about being too busy and needing client sessions to be transcribed led Beverly to volunteer. In her kindness this was how we started to work together, her doing transcriptions for me, which ultimately lead to us partnering up and using her personal sessions to develop this book you are reading.

I also wanted to point out that we don't just have our own personal spirit guides looking out for us. As Timingo has shown here with his pep talk letter to Beverly, he's letting her know that he too is on her side and has a vested interest in her life and her successes. So you too reader, have a lot more help than you ever were aware of!

This book started with Beverly and my un-celebrated first meeting, and now our partnership in authorship similarly was un-celebrated...I guess it was all planned that way!

Final Words

Beverly's Personal Journey Summary:

I categorized myself as an open-minded, progressive-leaning, traditional Protestant normie who rejected the gruesome concept of hell. My "Aha!" moments in broadening my view began when reading the Edgar Cayce literature decades ago. Finally, I had a tool to make all my unanswered church teachings fall into alignment for a more reasonable belief system.

Covered in this first book is the broad view of the years from 2009 to 2013. On the surface, I went from intense grief downwards to being crestfallen, slogging through more and more depression, all the while being bombarded by heavy, discouraging, troublesome entities. I couldn't identify or resist them, or even toss them out of my mind long enough to figure out an action plan.

Kym rescued me when she cracked open the door to the other side with its illuminating light. Only then was I slowly, gently exposed to the reasons under the surface layer for this particular spiritual journey of mine. I realize confronting my intense grief was the trigger to my spiritual growth, to my psychic abilities, and to the teachings of this invisible structure.

When I read the transcripts now, I'm stunned to see how weak and deflated I was. Time after time I asked the same questions in these sessions simply because I was unable to absorb the information while fighting to stay afloat with the voices.

Timingo was right. I didn't have the basic foundational background to comprehend how to use the good advice suggested. From the beginning, when voices, different from the voice of my own thoughts and internal dialogue, gradually could be heard in my head, I was puzzled. Next I was frightened, and then, mentally I ran away to hide in the corner.

Previously concealed, I didn't know my past lives and soul fragments could still speak of their old unresolved issues. Nor did I understand there were additionally some frustrated ghosts and entities in hell with the ability and desire to harangue me into helping them.

Added to that turbulent mix were friendly crossed-over spirits, including my spirit guides, who were giving me encouraging pep talks. Rereading the sessions, I now see all kinds of keywords and suggestions designed by my spirit guide, family, and friends to catapult me further along and out of my fearful interpretation of what I was experiencing. At the time, however, if their calm voices weren't drowned out by the pushy negative voices, I, in my ignorance, shut down *all* voices, including those from supportive spirits.

Mistakenly, I first thought I was an innocent victim, by a fluke of random circumstance, who confounded our Western medical system. In response, I victimized myself with my judgments and fears. I knew something was wrong. I hadn't lost me, yet there were many times when I dropped the reins of the decision-making process. My critical, immediate task, even when in the depths of despair, was to pick up those reins again and guide myself onto the course I wanted.

Had I known there existed six cast-of-character roles a soul can inhabit, I would have more quickly understood that these entity types all had different motives and thus predictable actions. Sorting out each voice by category and dealing with them independently was my job, my challenge. I read and reread the sessions many times, because each time I did, more strands of my life began to fall peacefully into place.

I believe if I had had this advanced knowledge thoroughly absorbed, I would not have sunk deeper and deeper into despair. For that reason I'm adamant about writing this first book so others with similar manifestations can work through their problem faster and easier than I did.

Thankfully, the learning continues as Kym and I work on more books in the *Soul Evolution: The Invisible Structure* series.

As you, the reader, reflect on your life's journey, don't make my same mistakes in your own life. Slow down your judgment calls regarding this type of experience while remaining open to all the other mysteries in this lifetime. If you can't see or hear what other folks do, don't assume they are wrong any more than you assume a color-blind person is wrong because he can't spot red or green. We all come equipped with different abilities. Some abilities are physical, some of them are psychic, either natural or developed. Our challenge is to bring forth the best in all of us.

As it turned out, my journey at the close of this book frequently found me overwhelmed by mean spirited voices insisting on ruling the roost. When I grew faint from the abuse, a loving force was on standby as an advocate. I survived those days with some improved hearing and discernment. *Thankfully.*

I invite you to reread and study this book's contents as an aid, a tool, and a comfort on your path.

— Beverly Hafemeister

Kym's Professional Journey Summary:

In this book I have taken on the role of sideline commentator/teacher, helping to explain and connect the dots for you, the reader. I did not want to take on that role. I was concerned that our readership would think I had all the answers, and I felt I didn't know enough. I didn't want to be perceived as an expert on these topics, because I saw myself learning right along side Bev. So how could I teach anyone?

It's true I knew a lot about psychic ability. Over 15 years as a professional medium, I listened as Timingo taught me while working with my clients. In the first draft of this book I took the role as someone just on the journey stating how cool all the new information was. But it took our editor to convince me that it was my job to bring my teaching ability to the book. The book needed it; the reader needed it. But it was scary and hard to step into those shoes. I had to find the courage to go through another transformation from experiencer to explainer and put on my big girl panties. It was the right move, and I hope the reader agrees.

The truth is, we wanted to write a book that transformed our readers because we had been transformed at the time of the teachings. We never thought that we would *continue transforming* just by simply writing these teachings for our readers and delving into our separate perspectives. We have grown and transformed over and over again as we worked on reviewing and clarifying the teaching for the written word (which is much different than the spoken word).

Beverly's changes were more obvious to me, since with each re-write she dug deeper and deeper into the events of those early years with the voices. In the sections of the "Beverly's Mindset" and "Beverly's Personal Journey," she revealed thoughts and feelings she never shared with me at the time. Reader, you need to remember, I was just a hired hand. I just answered the phone and gave the messages and hung up. There was no other contact except what you read in the book. We left nothing out. So much she never shared with me. Our rewrites made her dig deeper into a very scary past, filled with things she didn't want to resurrect. Our first draft was fluff compared to the richness of the last draft. I'm sure if she hadn't worked on this book, those ignored feelings and experiences would have added to her unfinished business in this life and would have caused her more work in future lives. I'm happy she was able to sort through these events in the same life she had experienced them.

On another note, in what we have just learned in this first book, I've come to understand life is much more complex than I have previously understood it to be. Some of you might be feeling the same frustration I felt when I, too, learned of the influence of life themes, unhealed issues of past lives, soul fragment feelings, ghosts, and spirits. I was weighed down by just the thought of all this interference. Wasn't life hard enough without adding more things to deal with? Ugh!

As I processed the material, I saw it explained some of the complicated feelings I was personally wrestling with. Seeing my issues from a new perspective allowed me to think about my life in ways I had never contemplated before. Some of this information may have seemed a bit out there to me, but why would I not investigate? If I looked at these influencing factors differently, could it help me solve my earthly problems quicker and without so much upheaval? Could it give me greater understanding of myself and my fellow man?

A real surprise, I discovered I had beliefs about things that I never knew I had. For instance, I found I had a strong belief about ghosts. This greatly surprised me because consciously, I don't recall ever thinking about ghosts. As I stated in the book, I didn't even believe ghosts were real. As we continually worked with the ghosts in the book, I uncovered other hidden beliefs I had about them. I believed they were stuck, which implied they "did something wrong."

I was deeply confused. If I had hidden beliefs about ghosts, what more pertinent beliefs did I hold on other topics? Things that directly affected my daily life? I found throughout this book I was always uncovering other beliefs that were taught to me by my childhood religion and my family and found that I was being challenged to investigate these beliefs to see if they were still true for me? Or were they outdated? Or just plain false? This book title clearly states I had many wrong beliefs about death and the grieving process. I was all wet about the heaven concept and I was gobsmacked by the hell topic and I was blown out of the water on my limiting judgmental beliefs about mental illness. I hope you, the reader, uncovered some of your limiting beliefs that you might have had on these subjects and other topics that our teachers brought up in these conversations. I challenge you to dig deep and investigate these hidden life motivators.

As I started to experiment with this new thinking, I found answers regarding the motivation of my own reactions and behaviors that I had never understood before. I felt relieved and recharged, with a renewed passion to engage in my life in ways I had always been afraid to do. My fears of death became nonexistent. My fears of things that go bump in the night didn't scare the wits out of me anymore. I no longer felt alone and left out to dry by life's circumstances. I quit judging and beating up on myself, and best of all, I quit being a victim of my life. I calmed down and took control of life.

The interactions with Beverly, Timingo, Bob/Cherith, Hal, Eleanor, Ray, Aunt Louise, and all the ghosts who talked with us, gave me insight into the complexities of life, and more personally, my life.

My greatest wish for you, dear reader, is that you earnestly seek out a conscious working relationship with your spirit guide. They are chomping at the bit to connect with you in a conscious way to assist, and teach you about your journey just like they did with Beverly and me. My life was irrevocably changed when I met Timingo. I wish that for each and every one of you, too.

We would, also, challenge you to read and then re-read this book over and over again and answer the questions we offer at the end of each chapter for deep reflection. These lessons are like an onion, they keep peeling away new insights which causes one to transform.

In book two in this series, the extraordinary journey continued with Bev being accosted by the voices. Our training was kicked into high gear, we :

- are taken deeper into the purposes of personal hells.
- are saddened to hear more details of the struggles that Beverly's mom endured and that led to the suicides of herself and others. We learned a lot about suicide and our misconceptions.
- have a visit and a teaching from another famous character from history about "What is a soul?" with a vivid rollercoaster ride of experience.
- have more ghost crossings. In the interviews with the ghosts, they reveal more about their purpose and experiences on that level.

And … we find out again how *We Got It All Wrong*.

— Kym McBride

Prelude To Book 2

This is a glimpse into a 3 day event that happened after book one ended. Kym did an experiment with Timingo, who gave insight into some things that happened in book one, so we included those insights to help you, reader. Now you know "the rest of the story" (quote of Paul Harvey)

June 28, 2013, Kym's Mindset:

Today I'm at Beverly's home to work on some parts of our book. We had scheduled a session where Beverly would interview Timingo *through* me, but I awoke with a slightly different idea of how to do this interview.

Way back in 2009, out of the blue, Timingo offered me a new experience. He thought this new teaching would give me a new perspective on the topic of possession. I was open for it and before I knew it, he slipped into my body. He wiggled inside me, *with me*, as if my body were a glove, a tightly fitting glove.

It was very odd. Timingo controlled the right side of my body and I had the left side. I could not raise my right hand or move my right leg. While in this situation, I decided I wanted a cup of coffee, but walking to the kitchen felt like an awkward three legged race. We each struggled to control our own side of the body and wobbled wildly from side to side.

While the coffee was brewing, I noticed the dirty dishes in the sink. Since he had control of my right hand, I asked Timingo if he could help me wash them. I was so preoccupied by how this body possession felt to me that I hadn't gotten around to wondering what Timingo might be feeling.

When I turned on the hot water with my left hand, he placed his controlled right hand under the running water and kept it there. I asked, "What are you doing?"

He sighed, "I have never felt hot running water before. It's very pleasant."

I never considered that this might be an entirely new experience for him since his last time in a body was in the 15th century! "Oh, that's right. You had no running hot water back in your day! But you have seen me wash dishes hundreds of times, right?"

He said, "Yes, but seeing and feeling are two completely different experiences. I like washing dishes."

I snorted a laugh, "Well, I hate washing dishes. If you want to take over that job, it's fine with me!"

After a cup of coffee and letting him feel more simple actions of being in my body, I was done with the teaching experience and told Timingo to get out. He cautioned me that exiting my body would be harder on me than entering. He would have to do it slowly. I felt him remove himself part by part: his head, one arm, one leg, and so forth. Once fully out, my body collapsed. I struggled to get to my bed. Instantaneously, I fell into a deep, long nap only to awaken feeling hung over because his energy didn't mix well with mine. I told Timingo it was an interesting exercise, but once was enough, thank you very much!

Now today, four years later, I awoke with an idea. Maybe it's time to try body possession again, but this time completely vacate my body and leave it in Timingo's hands. With this method I can watch Beverly interview Timingo directly without me being a participant. I figured I'd ask Timingo what he thinks.

As I was making my morning coffee, I asked, "Timingo, are you here?"

He said, "Yes, of course, Fine One."

I asked, "How about we do this interview session today a little differently? I want *you* to talk directly to Beverly using your words and inflections not mine. I want to be out of the way. Can I get up, leave my body, and go sit over on the steps while you and Beverly visit on the porch?"

Timingo laughed, "If I recall, you didn't like it the last time I was in your body. We can do it this way if you wish, but we don't need to."

I said, "I think I would like to give it a try."

It was time to begin the session. I feel his energy getting in me. It's a little snug at first. Then I did as Timingo had demonstrated in 2009. I started to step out of the body, piece by piece. It was absolutely freeing!

I was now a translucent image of myself. I walked over to the porch steps and sat down. I looked back to the chair on the porch and also saw my body sitting there strong and upright. It was freaky. I tried to move the hand of the body in the chair, but it didn't move. I was completely unable to control that body, but I still *felt* it.

What I hadn't known or anticipated was that my brain would become mush. I lost control of it. I could hear Beverly and Timingo talking, but was unable to understand the conversation. I wasn't scared, just annoyed. As the session went on, I started to comprehend bits and pieces, but I couldn't hold onto any word or thought for more than a nanosecond.

I was unable to talk. My translucent mouth moved, but nothing came out. Then I realized Timingo could hear me telepathically, but I couldn't hear a telepathic reply from him. Only when Timingo, in the loaner body, answered my question or statement out loud did I know he had heard me. As time went on, I started to get some control over my mind again. I finally was able to make an intelligent statement, but many times Timingo would not give up the floor to my input.

It's funny. He was reluctant to do this experiment, but when I wanted to join the conversation, Timingo didn't want to give up control!

Here's what happened next:

Beverly (B), Kym (K), and Timingo (T)

B: Let's begin. Good morning, Timingo. If you're comfortably settled in, may I start with my questions about the letter you dictated to Kym for me on May 16, 2013?

T: If you like, let's go there. I'm at your disposal.

B: I underlined the phrase *earth plane and beyond*. The *beyond* is a puzzle. I guessed it was the sleep stage.

T : No, you guessed wrong. I was referring to the ghost experience. As you learn about the ghost area and communicate this understanding to the masses, we will open up what's on the other side of the light. You both don't understand it completely. When Kym crosses ghosts, she creates a doorway emanating a bright inviting light and sees people meeting their loved ones. In her vernacular it's heaven, but it's not heaven, just another level.

We're hoping within this lifetime which you two share together, there will be time to teach these other levels. First, you have to learn about the ghost level which is the foundation for the next level. This knowledge will help you see the beginning structure of how a soul evolves through an organized pattern. Then, you can share this *invisible structure* with other people.

B: Wonderful. Your letter said that my work has been so much more than I have been aware. What does that mean?

T: When in the hospital, you were brought to the depths of what you were calling craziness, yet we, your guides, were just acknowledging your scheduled plan of "going low enough, depressed enough, strung out enough, desperate enough to get to the level of helping the souls trapped in their personal hells."

Beverly, for the first time, you consciously began to feel like one of the souls trapped in hell. Previously, you were unaware of both this kind of work and your participation in it. This is breakthrough information for you! Look at this work from a military frame of mind …

Leaders need to know how their soldiers will react to a surprise attack, so officials devise a learning exercise where every soldier uses his training and his wits to figure out how to react to events he thinks are real.

In your case, that's what happened. Unaware, you were dropped into a planned artificial event. You didn't know it was an exercise before, during, and even long after the experience was over.

B: Well, just the little bit of knowledge I've gained on this topic has helped me.

T: You literally have this much knowledge. [*Timingo holds up his thumb and finger, indicating a slim space between them*] If it's caused you to have some relief, can you imagine when true knowing comes in? Then, you can control fear and make decisions. But see, you're not at that level yet, therefore, we can't even discuss details much. I don't want to bring fear up in you.

Your fear, these walls you've put around yourself, will start to come down little by little as you get more and more knowledge of spiritual growth and the process of all souls. All in due time, all in due time. You will have your answers as to how you do what you do.

B: May I talk a minute about being fear-blocked which you mentioned in your letter? My response is that I didn't know I was! When I was in the hospital and just before, I didn't understand my head was actually a battlefield where I was getting conflicting messages from at least two different sources. I was very slow to catch on. Every word I was hearing in my head I believed was religiously from *on high.* Yet, some of it was foolish and some of it was incorrect. Strangely, because I believed the messages came from *on high*, I didn't know and it never occurred to me that I was supposed to filter out nonsense. I began to feel like a passenger in my own life, not the driver. Now, I feel helplessness is a big factor in my fears.

T: Let's see if I, along with your guide who's talking to me, can explain this properly. "You're working for God, for the greater, clearer light. You're going through this earthly experience with a Godly purpose," as Kym says. All humans are, they're just unaware of it.

Beverly, you're just becoming aware of having three different experiences in one life. First, you're having an Earth life, with the need to evolve as a person, like everyone else. Second, you're helping souls cross out of their personal hells. And third, you've taken on studying a higher level of understanding about the evolution of your soul, while at the same time you're also trying to teach it to other people on Earth.

What I referenced in my letter was the fact that you were never alone. You were far enough along on your spiritual path to know you couldn't access the answers for your grief. You knew to ask yourself, "Where can I seek help?"

Eventually, you turned to Kym with her connection to me and your guide, so you received the answers you sought for your grief. But it opened you up to other challenges which *didn't* help you at first. You *didn't* have the foundation for assimilating the information!

Now, three years later, you're not the same person with that limitation. You've learned more about discernment to help you continue to do the work—your night work and these books. During each session with us you acquired more tools to better your skills. You will not fall for such gross misdirection again.

B: When I was in the hospital, I remember popping awake in the mornings feeling fine. I figured I was in a good place while I slept. Of course, when I opened my eyes, the chatter immediately started up.

T: Your two worlds were colliding, which caused all your confusion. However, they had to collide for you to become conscious of the work you do at night. Can we call it an ugly transition where two things awkwardly come together? As Kym says, "Transitions are not pretty for a while."

B: Yeah, I feel I'm shutting off voices I don't want to hear. I'm starting to catch on that I need to identify who is whom.

T: Yes, your discernment is getting bigger and better. You're not falling into being prey for souls desperately trying to get your attention. Never fear, your guides are always in council with you.

B: So now they'll help me better understand my experience?

T: Yes, you won't be so afraid of it. We want you to experience on a level where your *knowing* comes in, not just having to trust what Kym and I tell you. We feel coping with ghosts and souls with Kym will help to dissipate some of those fears. Then we can start to educate you in the depth of your own work.

B: I'm assuming I'll be doing this in future lives, too?

T: Yes, let me clarify. You've been doing it in past lives, but unconsciously and in great peril to yourself. You have not yet been able to get past fear to grasp the true knowledge of events.

B: What does "great peril" mean? Like my mother's suicide?

T: Exactly.

B: I was afraid of that. I'd like to switch the conversation now to our massive crossing of souls in April. Several things happened which puzzled us, perhaps you can clarify matters.

In some previous group crossings, like Savannah, Kym noticed ghosts were crossing over by era or by occupation. In other words, they sort themselves into categories. Yet, here in April, they appeared to be randomly lined up. Is there some significance?

T: There really is! I know Kym wondered, but she never asked me directly so we never made time to talk about her keen observation. It's the cultural location of a particular place. In the South, they divide into social class.

On the other hand, with the major crossing here in Ohio, categorizing by social class orientation isn't important. Protocol in Cincinnati is unlike Savannah or elsewhere. The prominent etiquette and thought energy of a location dictates how spirits line up. See, every place has an energy and a belief system which permeates the soil and space, hence, it's an example of *stratified energy*.

B: Oh, that's interesting! Let me think about that later. Back to the questions … On our recording of the April crossing I heard myself crying when Kym said something like, "Do you feel the happiness?" Do you remember that incident? What triggered my tears?

T: Yes, Kym accurately interpreted that emotion was rolling in. Beverly, visualize a picture of energy as a semisolid force, looking like a cloud. Energy rolled in and hit you all, and you reacted to being hit by this emotion energy, but you didn't know what the emotion was. Kym labeled it happiness, but it was really *relief*. A rolling cloud of relief was for the ghosts who had waited so long on this level. It was to let them know this experience would soon be over. Happy, excited, joyous relief. It is similar to the relief Earth people feel when they die and discard the weight of their earthly body.

You reacted to the feeling of that energy by crying, not knowing what it was.

B: Okay then. Shortly thereafter, probably it was Kym who said, "Yes, it's here," in reply to the ghosts asking "Is *it* here?" What did the people mean by *it*?

T: Opportunity. The light was here. Here was an opportunity to exit off of the ghost plane, the vehicle for them to get relief. So, *it* was good terminology because there were fifty, sixty, seventy belief systems involved in that event. *It* fit into all their definitions.

Kym's intent was a bright, white-lit doorway, but each ghost's perception was an individual image. Some men might see saloon doors, others might see church doors, but each saw it as a good door. However, not everyone sees a door. One person might see God, another person might see colors. As in all events, on Earth or in spirit, it's always a personal experience of creating.

B: I was greatly touched by the dramatic story of the group of nuns. Can you give us more of their backstory? On the ghost plane, how were they able to shed their shame?

T: Yes, that particular group carried the stigma of being raped and murdered, along with other atrocities they experienced and witnessed in life. Their problem wasn't forgiving their rapists and murderers; that was easy for them; they couldn't forgive themselves for not knowing, not seeing, not being aware they were vulnerable.

On the ghost level, the nuns, as a group, decided to be around other women on Earth who were dealing with these same issues in a different format. Over the years these ghost nuns actually were drawn to women's shelters here on Earth. The nuns learned about their own unhealed feelings through the compassionate counseling shown towards the women in these shelters. They grew to understand they didn't make or have a choice in their experience, so why should they have shame?

While in one shelter, the nuns were in the midst of a group counseling session where they learned through watching Tamara, a young black woman who had been raised to believe that women were beholden to men. Tamara became property of a man who repeatedly abused her. When she finally got out of that situation, the nuns watched Tamara progress through counseling by analyzing: What was her part of being in a relationship? What was his part? What was their behavior together?

Although Tamara was not raped by a stranger like the nuns, they learned from her growth and new awareness. By being a compassionate group, the nuns made a huge leap forward by helping each nun through the healing process of letting go of the shame. As a unit they healed quicker than they would have as individuals.

Now as healed nuns, they in turn energetically assisted other abused women struggle with not forgiving themselves in these abusive relationships. This is how souls on the ghost level have a positive impact on people who are living.

And, Beverly, you have a bit of that self-imposed shame directed at yourself. Not a judgment, just an awareness.

B: Yes. Shame is a kissing cousin to self-loathing. It's one of my top priorities these days.

At this crossing, another ghost who really endeared himself to me was Ferdinand, my great grandfather, who asked to join the group of us holding hands. How sweet of him to want to assist! Why did my mother say no?

T: His energy and this experience were not in alignment. The power needed to cross over so many ghosts would have been broken. In order to be in alignment with the group which was brought together, he needed to make the shift out of the dense energy of his ghostly form.

The order of density from heavy to light energy is humans, then ghosts, then crossed-over spirits. Hal, your mom, and your uncle are crossed-over spirits who are at the next level. Before crossing-over, Ferdinand, a ghost, is incapable of elevating his energy high enough to assist, which has nothing to do with being good enough.

Joining the circle at that moment would have distracted from the overall needs of that day. You three live humans, who are the densest of all, had to raise your own internal energy to try to make that transition. It takes practice to be able to raise your internal energy. Kym and Mary were accustomed to doing that so they helped you.

B: That description helps me to visualize what was going on, thanks. Another shocking surprise that day was when Kym apparently saw what I believe was Aunt Carrie …

T: It was.

B: Okay. When Aunt Carrie headed towards the light, my mother, who was in our circle, split and went to the entrance of the light. Kym said she'd never seen a spirit split before. Do you want to elaborate?

T: Well, a spirit is energy, and it can split itself. Kym hasn't had the visual awareness of that trait before. All this splitting has been happening before, but she wasn't able to see it. This day she made an enormous leap into different abilities! She was able to see multiple people, all at the same time, from live humans to crossed spirits and ghosts. She had never seen as clearly as she did on that day.

She usually has to focus for each group in a different way. This time they were right there in different parts of the room. She was finally able to perceive it all, even to catch sight of ghosts in the dining room, ghosts standing on the steps, and awareness of the ghosts standing behind her.

Furthermore, she had never worked before with crossed-over spirits who joined the circle to add energy as assistants in a mass crossing of ghosts.

All that experience was profound in her teaching. Yet, she lost the memory of a lot of the details because so many things were simultaneously happening. In reviewing this written material, I'm hoping more awareness will return to her.

I would like to note here about the ghosts standing behind Kym. Remember, ghosts can overhear conversations and learn from them. For example, the two sisters who wanted to carry in their headstone shared their fear that they would turn to dust if they walked into the light. By questioning this fear, the girls were helping the shame-filled ghosts who also had this same fear. So in talking with Kym, they learned this was a false teaching and not going to happen. These shame-filled ghosts, learned something new in watching this exchange, hence growth. Sadly, religions can be great teachers of shame.

One key point I want you and Kym to take away from this mass crossing, which I don't feel you were able to catch in the discussion with the nuns, was Kym's important question, "Why did an entire group of nuns become ghosts?" One woman replied, "They had died in shame from being raped, but they had dealt with their shame on this ghost level."

It was a turning point for many reluctant shame-filled ghosts standing in the gallery behind Kym. That one simple, inquisitive question stunned a new awakening to that specific audience.

They internalize, "Does this means while here I can heal the issue that caused me to become a ghost so I, too, can then go into the light?" This simple new idea changed their view of the ghostly experience from their perception of it being a punishment to being a learning opportunity.

Kym's providing a great service beyond what she realizes, since she was educating this specific group of ghosts who were struggling with shame.

Something you both need to know is that *ghosts actually learn and grow on the ghost level.* This area of training is going to be a focus in our subsequent sessions. Much misinformation is perpetuated by TV and movies. We can't wait to share this new awareness with you both.

End Session

[*For all those concerned, Kym was able to take her body back.*]

Be sure to check out the companion workbook on *We Got It All Wrong: death and grief, heaven and hell, and mental illness*, which will be available January 2017.

For more information about the second book in this series, sit tight until Fall of 2017.

Acknowledgements

Beverly Hafemeister:

I am in awe of the mediumship skill of Kym McBride, my co-author and fellow seeker, who has made my journey so powerfully revealing of its problems and Source-directed solutions. I thank her, plus a tip of my hat to her sidekick Timingo, for sharing their great gifts with me.

Writing this book, at times, has been a gut wrenching experience to look deeply for any ugliness to be swept out. I'm grateful for the countless scores of helpers on the other side who patiently urged me to be of courage and good cheer to do the necessary work to toss out my unneeded baggage. I'm deeply touched by the many signs of your love.

I wish also to thank the inspiring volunteers who helped with the development of our book as Alpha Testers: Theresa Bost, Carolyn DeAngelis, Wendy Fedan, Ron Frazer, Tammy Goyke, Diane Hofmann, Sara McDonough, Carissa Rowe, Suzanne Scott, Mary Simpson, and Mary Svoboda. Helpful human hands are every bit as wonderful as hands on the other side! Many thanks for your dedication.

To the readers, may the information in this book bring renewed awe and God's peace.

Acknowledgements

Kym McBride:

First, I have to thank my partner in crime, Beverly. I cannot imagine a better partner in writing this series of books. Not only is she the hardest worker (she would give the EverReady Bunny a run for his money) but she has shouldered the passion to keep this enormous series moving forward. I take my hat off to her!

Next, I have to give the biggest kiss to my BFF Mary Svoboda. She also possesses *super powers* of being a great listener. She sits through the endlessly chatter and details about my latest project, because I have to process everything outside myself. She is always ready to jump into a new adventures with me of which many are peppered throughout this book and series. I can't believe that we found each other in this cluttered world.

Our largest support in getting our book to market was by the generous help of our three editors at PaperRavenBooks.com, Morgan, Jennifer, and Chris. Our in-house line editor, "the Savant" Tammy Goyke and our formatter Ron Frazer helped ease the pain of keeping all the plates spinning. I send a big kiss to each and everyone of you!

And lastly, I want to thank my first husband (he hates being call my ex) John Dravecky. I can't say he has been overly supportive with this series; he doesn't get my obsession, but he is the BESTIE in my life. John, I love you with all my heart and I'm so glad we divorced so I could keep loving you and not kill you.

Author Bio: Beverly Hafemeister

"What do you think Bev's really doing when she walks down to the lake and spends hours there?"

Not surprised by the question from her color-blind husband, Beverly's sister responded, "Well, she's an artist! She loves the panoramic skyscape and all the nuances of blue in the lake."

Sis could have added the sight of leisurely sailboats luffing in the wind and loaded Lake Michigan cargo ships headed into port; or the craggy, moss covered stone steps winding down from the lake bluff past wild flowers under sentinel trees. This lovely little park, occasionally enjoyed by excited dogs plopping into the water from a forlorn jetty to retrieve sticks tossed into the lake by their owners, is a source of visual delights and deep musings for me, Beverly.

I crave beauty. As I unraveled my journey for you, you probably began to understand my internal struggle to find serene loveliness from an ugly, chaotic situation.

Author Bio: Kym McBride

Kym is a psychic, medium, mentor, teacher, author, yada yada yada. Which means she talks *a lot!* But it works well with her Gemini communication personality. She is bold and direct and doesn't mince words. (YIKES!) This is her first published work, but she has forty-seven more projects in the queue. Let's hope she finishes them before she's dead. She is a self-professed workaholic.

She has been living on the lam for almost 15 years, including living in South America and Ireland. She is madly in love with her bright green VW bug and binge watching Netflix. She prides herself on never having to leave the house because more action happens there with all the dead people popping in! She's only forced to leave the house when *the TP runs out*. She is single and *not* looking...except for a dog. Oh, and she hates serious bio's.

Find more of Kym at ClearingTheCrap.com and KymMcBride.com.

Glossary

We have included a list of words and topics that are used throughout the book. These definitions are based on Kym's and Beverly's understandings taught by their guides. After each term, the listed chapter is where the word was first introduced.

Please note: *that some words are used throughout the book, but only the chapter it was first introduced is listed and not each subsequent chapter where it appeared.*

Akashic Record: (chapter 2) The energetic history of all life, which is essentially a universal super-computer, storing every deed, word, feeling, thought, and intention that has ever manifested in history with each individual soul. These records exist for every soul who has ever existed.

Aura: (chapter 6) A colorful multi-level energy field that surrounds the body of a living person, thing or place. This energy is generated by the thing it surrounds. This energy is imprinted with knowledge about the health, feelings, and blocks that person/thing/place has.

Belief Clusters: (chapter 9) Out of body souls are magnetically drawn together because of a *shared* belief system.

Channeling: (chapter Navigate) *In reference to channeling through mediumship*. Mediums can channel the dead. They can pick up feelings, personality, words, and many times actual inflections of the person's style of speaking as well as their physicality.

Charge: (chapter 1) A human who has been assigned a mentor, who is a crossed over spirit. (This is in addition to a spirit guide.)

Chill: (chapter Navigate) A chill or electrical charge that originates from the inside of a person to the outside, similar to the physical experience of goosebumps. This physical manifestation is a validation that a message has been understood correctly or the statement made was true. This can happen to professional psychics or to lay people alike.

Clairaudience: (chapter 4) A type of psychic ability. The person hears sounds or voices or information that are inaudible to others.

Clairvoyant: (chapter Navigate) A type of psychic ability. The person perceiving beyond the regular five senses and has the ability to see into one's past and future.

Crossed spirit: (chapter Navigate) A deceased person who has gone through the light and entered the other side of existence.

Dreams: (chapter 1) A tool that spirits and spirit guides use to impart information to a sleeping person. Dreams use assorted types of symbols and metaphors to convey information.

Enlightenment: (chapter Navigate) Enlightenment equals the collection of knowledge. This knowledge once implemented into a person's life/beliefs/behaviors allows them to advance through the transition into higher levels of awareness.

Essence: (chapter 7) An energetic characteristic that emulates from a person that is felt by other humans.

Ghosts: (chapter Navigate) Deceased humans who have not crossed over through the light to the other side. They are on this ghost level to continue healing the issues they didn't resolve before their death.

Ghost whisperer: (chapter Navigate) Another type psychic ability has be dubbed ghost whisperers *(after the TV show of the same name)*. They are not psychic (seeing the future) and can not see crossed-over spirits. Their ability lies in seeing earthbound ghosts and helping them to cross into the light.

Hell: (chapter 10) A large or small pocket of space a spirit decides to create to contain themselves. It's an illusionary world or situation to punish *themselves* after death.

Hell-work: (chapter 10) Living souls who volunteer to join the Warrior team to rescue deceased spirits who have imprisoned themselves in their own personal hell. The concept of warrior teams will be expanded in Book 2.

Invisible structure: (chapter Navigate) An organized, multifaceted format one follows for the evolution of their soul to lead them back to Source.

Knowing: (chapter Navigate) A type of psychic ability. It can't be taught, it just happens where information pops into your head about someone or something. There are no visions, or voices to tell you this information, it just pops in; you just seem to know.

Light: (chapter Navigate) A light that is created to allow a dead soul to exit one level of existence into another level that involves different awareness.

Life theme: (chapter 2) A pre-determined theme a soul chooses to experience in a variety of ways while the soul moves through their life on Earth. The chief topic a soul chooses to experience in their current life. This theme is the filter the soul looks through when experiencing everything.

Life Between Life Review: (chapter 11) The close analysis of your recent life with your spirit guide and counselors as an aid in understanding deeply about the events of that life. This information is used in planning your next journey.

Medium: (chapter Navigate) A psychic with the additional ability to channel dead people. Mediums receive communication through their senses; touch, sight, hearing, taste, smell, and knowing.

Normie: (chapter 4) People who are not aware of the spiritual side of their existence. They believe existence is all about dealing with the physical side of life: getting a job, getting married, picking up the children from school, paying bills. They are consumed with this illusion and not aware of all the unseen elements happening around them—blissfully unaware.

Outline: (chapter 1) A detailed plan of how a soul will return to the Earth level and advance through this multi-level, invisible structure to bring their soul back to their God-self as they gain experience and knowledge.

Obsession: (chapter 6) A ghost invades a living person's *aura* looking for the familiarity of living in a body. They can influence that human's thoughts without the person even being aware of it.

Possession: (chapter 6) A ghost invades the *physical body* of another human to seek control and live in the body once more. This ghost can control a living being through throughs and actions. This can happen without a person being aware of it.

Psychic: (chapter Navigate) Perceiving beyond the regular five senses. A person who can channel information from your spirit guides and others about your past and future.

Soul cluster: (chapter Navigate) Spiritually related humans descended from the same soul; create a group/custer. These soul cluster members can feel and react to their other soul members' situations, often completely unaware they are feeling another's feelings.

Soul fragments: (chapter Navigate) Human portions of the same soul.

Source: (chapter Navigate) The supreme being, whatever you chose to call it.

Spirits: (chapter Navigate) A general term to encapsulate all souls when not in a body; regardless of their level.

Spirit guides: (chapter Navigate) A specific soul with experience as a human assigned to be a companion to a soul that is on their journey while the soul is both in and out of that human body.

Stratified Energy: (chapter Prelude) Energy that has a way of organizing itself into layers such as cultural social levels. For example: the thought and belief patterns of a country, state, city or group can be so strong that those patterns impregnate the culture of the individuals and societies—even the soil of an area. We were surprised to learn that these patterns can survive death.

The other side: (chapter Prologue) This is a generalized term to describe the post-Earth location for spirits. Sometimes thought of as home or heaven, but is really just someplace that is not Earth.

Twilight links: (chapter 10) All living people can leave their bodies when they sleep. In the bodiless form once asleep they can travel to visit other alive people and interact, like a "Meet up" in sleep! Some sensitive people can recall these twilight visits and some can't.

Vision: (chapter Navigate) An image that pops into a psychic's head. It appears like a TV show which a psychic watch's then describes to the client. But, the psychic is also interpreting information from that TV show.

Warriors: (chapter Navigate) A generalized term for a team of souls (alive and dead) who have volunteered to help rescue troubled spirits who have created for themselves a personal hell illusion into which they cannot escape. The concept of warrior teams will be expanded in Book 2.

Story Index

Messages are remembered by their stories

Chapter 1 Dr. Jack Kevorkian Dr. Bruce Lipton	**Chapter 8** Outline Quintuplets Mary and Roman
Chapter 2 Dr. Brian Greene Big and little orbs The White Brotherhood Harry Emerson Fosdick	**Chapter 9** Ernest Hemingway (Hemmy) Mary and ghosts in the cemetery Belief Cluster
Chapter 3 Past life as miracle child Mattie Stepanek	**Chapter 10** Releasing mementos *What Dreams May Come* (movie) Tim apology
Chapter 4 Father, daughter, and death levels Tim and Hal Hints from Heloise	**Chapter 11** Life between Life Review Earth Spirit Daniel Robber story
Chapter 5 Ellie and the ghost's request	**Chapter 12** Beverly's family ghosts Single crossing of Uncle Art
Chapter 6 Jesus explains the different types of possession	**Chapter 13** Mass crossing Eleanor's energy splits Ferdinand, Aunt Louise Aunt Carrie and shame Emil Hafemeister
Chapter 7 Dreams: Swimming, Cargo Plane Art fair exhibitor Friar Girolamo Savonarola Essence: Red-haired churchman Repertory Thespians Soul Fragment: Church wall	**Prelude to Book 2** Timingo shares Kym's body Conclusion to ghost nun story

Thank you so much for purchasing:

We got It All Wrong: death and grief, heaven and hell, and mental illness

From our

Soul Evolution: the Invisible Structure series

As an added bonus we have prepared a *FREE* 30-page PDF companion workbook that you can use to work along as you read through the book.

GET WORKBOOK AT:
HTTP://BIT.LY/SESERIES

42325350R00171

Made in the USA
San Bernardino, CA
01 December 2016